DATE DUE

SEP 3 0 2003	
OCT 0 3 2003	
OCT 1 7 2003	
OCT 2 7 2003 NOV 0 3 2003	
NOV 1 4 2003	
NOV 2 4 2003 FEB 2 2 2006	
JUN 3 0 2006	
JUL 3 1 2006	
AUG 1 4 2006	
SEP 3 0 2006	
JY 11 07	

DEMCO, INC. 38-2931

WITHDRAWN

ALSO BY BARBARA WITT

George Foreman's Big Book of Grilling,
Barbecue, and Rotisserie
by George Foreman and Barbara Witt

Classic American Food Without Fuss:
Over 100 Favorite Recipes Made Easy
by Barbara Witt and Frances Monson McCullough

Pan-Asian Express: Quick Fixes for Asian-Food Fans
by Barbara Witt

Great Feasts Without Fuss: Professional Secrets
for Creating Carefree Dinner Parties
by Frances Monson McCullough and Barbara Witt

Great Food Without Fuss: Simple Recipes
from the Best Cooks
by Barbara Witt and Frances Monson McCullough

THE WEEKEND CHEF

192 Smart Recipes for
Relaxed Cooking
Ahead

BARBARA WITT

SIMON & SCHUSTER

New York London Toronto

Sydney Singapore

SIMON & SCHUSTER
Rockefeller Center
1230 Avenue of the Americas
New York, NY 10020

SIMON & SCHUSTER and colophon are registered trademarks of Simon & Schuster, Inc.

For information about special discounts for bulk purchases,
please contact Simon & Schuster Special Sales:
1-800-456-6798 or business@simonandschuster.com

Book design by Ellen R. Sasahara

Manufactured in the United States of America

1 3 5 7 9 10 8 6 4 2

Library of Congress Cataloging-in-Publication Data

Witt, Barbara.
The weekend chef : 192 smart recipes for relaxed cooking ahead / Barbara Witt.
p. cm.
Includes index.
1. Make-ahead cookery.   I. Title.
TX652.W625 2003
641.5'55—dc21   2003050584

ISBN 0-7432-2991-6

INTERIOR PHOTO CREDITS

Pages iii, viii, xiii, 30, 61: John Vorhes/The Vorhes Studio
Pages xiv, 7, 53, 76, 90, 156: Sandra Lousada
Page 54: Yuki Tatsumi
Page 79: Weston Konishi
Pages 20, 93: Charlie Sleichter
Pages 114, 171: Danny O'Shea
Page 181: Christian Grinschgl

Acknowledgments

Although cookbook publishers allot a page near the front of the book for the author's acknowledgments, I've never used it for the same reason that I click Mute on my remote during the Academy Awards thank-you speeches. It always seemed to me that thanking your parents for birthing you, your spouse for loving you, and your friends for being just that ought to be private, off-camera moments. On the other hand, one should probably grab any public opportunity that arises to display one's beneficence and, at the same time, totally embarrass a good friend and colleague.

So I've decided to embarrass Fran McCullough, editor extraordinaire and author of the justly acclaimed Best American Recipes cookbook series. Together, Fran and I have written three books, one of which won a James Beard award, but it isn't that collaboration alone that wins my gratitude. It goes all the way back to my unsolicited-manuscript submission to her when she sat on her deserved pedestal as senior cookbook editor at Harper & Row. I was invited to meet her for the first time at a trendy east-side New York City restaurant to discuss the publication of *The Big Cheese Cookbook,* based on the food I was serving in my Washington, D.C., restaurant at the time. I was a complete novice in the awesome world of publishing and pathetically nervous to meet one of its editorial icons. I could have spared myself the angst—Fran wasn't scary in the least.

Although I closed the restaurant before the book was complete, from that afternoon on Fran has been consistently supportive and encouraging while I wondered what on earth I was doing writing cookbooks at all. She knew my passion better than I. She was positive when I had qualms. She generously offered experienced advice when asked, recommended me to others, tossed interesting assignments my way, and was the kind of friend and cheerfully gracious mentor everyone should be lucky enough to have in one's life.

Thank you, Fran. I hope you like this one. It wouldn't have been possible without you.

Contents

Introduction

T his is my fourth attempt at writing the Introduction, which, I was told, no one reads anyway. Since, in that case, I was effectively talking to myself, I started off by railing against the wagon train of fast-food kitchens encircling our neighborhoods and threatening family unity by luring us from the hearth with their quick fixes and funky fries. I blamed the pizza delivery boy for the baby turtles housed in our stockpots and the sneakers drying in our ovens. I held the prolific carryout shops responsible for our lackluster diet of gummy pasta salads and incinerated chickens. I speculated that media-driven celebrity chefs in their signature whites, edgy restaurants serving over-the-top food, and dueling culinary magazines may have given home cooks a whale of a complex. Home cooks protest that there's no time for creative family cooking, let alone entertaining friends, but perhaps they just feel nothing they do will measure up. There was a time when the goal was to measure up to one's mom, but, even for today's younger grandmothers, that bib-aproned lady is all but a ghost.

Somewhere in one of those false starts I also wrote lyrically about cooking as a lifetime craft, as an art for the gifted few and always as a gift to the recipient. Not that dedicated cooks needed reminding of the creative and sensual rewards of their favorite hobby. From the rainbow panoply of the marketplace, through the pleasurable touch, discovery, and aroma, to the purring sounds around the table—cooking beats pulling garden weeds by a mile. I can think of no pastime more fulfilling in myriad ways than cooking. It may be a transitory pleasure for cook and diner alike, but memories of a good table can linger for a lifetime.

After a few pages of such reflective nattering came the epiphany. A cookbook introduction is supposed to introduce the book. So, to get back on track, this book is meant to speak to those who know and love good food and the pleasure of preparing it but have reluctantly succumbed to the workday pressure of putting dinner on the table right now. Surely such pressure trivializes the value of families joining at the communal dinner table. It's for those who, when they do manage to meter out a few hours in the kitchen, end up planning a special weekend dinner which, although undoubtedly appreciated, results mainly in a messy kitchen and an empty fridge. Weeknight pressure and nagging guilt remain.

What this book is *not* about is cooking on fast forward or creating six degrees of separation from a time-honored dish by subtracting every element of its flavor and complexity. It's a pity to sacrifice such dishes to a soccer game or the TV remote control. One solution is to deconstruct labor-intensive recipes into components that can be cooked and stored in your spare time and quickly assembled another day. A companion solution is to tackle complex dishes only when you can leisurely enjoy their preparation, choosing recipes that can be safely stored in the refrigerator or freezer. Another way to assure that a simple grilled fish or chop escapes mediocrity is to prepare complementary side dishes, condiments, sauces, and salsas ahead of time to enliven an otherwise dull meal. Any of these options will leave you with a stocked pantry.

My cabinets, refrigerator, and freezer all constitute my "pantry" and, in the best of months, they will be harmoniously stocked. Why defrost the pasta sauce if there's no dry pasta in the cupboard? The sautéed mixed mushrooms might taste great in a risotto, but is there Carnaroli rice? How can you make ginger caramel sauce without preserved ginger or a chocolate treat without the chocolate? It's frustrating to hunger for a quick Thai curry when there's no coconut milk. Every artist works from a varied paint palette and is inspired by different colors. What you keep on your culinary palette will naturally differ from mine, but it's wise to build a pantry that supports your personal creative style and spontaneity; otherwise, you're doomed to the tiresome short-order cooking we all strive to escape.

The few recipes selected for this book are purposely diverse—even a bit chaotic. Some are familiar, some hopefully not. They are meant merely to suggest the range of "keeper food" you can work back into your culinary repertoire. Once you embrace the underlying logic you and yours will be eating better and healthier. You'll revisit the rewards of an essential craft and help to perpetuate it through fond memory.

Above all, you'll cook again with pleasure, not pressure.

STOCKING THE PANTRY

If you have to make a big grocery run every time you're in the mood to cook, you're likely to trade in the whole idea for a good book. Building a well-stocked pantry takes time, and I'm sure much of what's on this list, culled from the recipes in this book, you already have at hand. Check off what's missing, begin collecting, so when you start weekend cooking regularly you'll only have to go out for a few fresh ingredients—remember, it's supposed to be a pleasure. Sorry, I have no suggestions for escaping the cleanup. The only pantry advice I can offer is to mark the month and year on every herb jar as you buy it. A year later they should really be ditched—some sooner than others. Take a good sniff and if they've lost their bright pungency, just let them go.

HERBS AND SPICES
Allspice
Bay leaves
Beau Monde seasoning
Cayenne pepper
Chili powder
Cinnamon, ground and whole
Cloves, ground and whole
Coriander, ground and whole
Cumin, ground and whole
Curry powder
Dill
Garam masala
Ginger, ground
Mint
Mustard, dry, Coleman's
Nutmeg, ground and whole
Oregano
Pepper, white, ground

Peppercorns, black
Pepper flakes, red
Saffron threads, Spanish
Salt, kosher
Thyme
Turmeric

EXTRACTS
Almond
Lemon
Pure vanilla

CONDIMENTS
Capers
Dijon mustard
Honey
Hot honey mustard
Horseradish
Ketchup

Maple syrup, pure
Mayonnaise, preferably Hellmann's or
 Best Foods
Tabasco sauce
Worcestershire sauce

OIL AND VINEGAR
Olive oil, cooking
Olive oil, extra-virgin
Safflower oil
Balsamic vinegar
Cider vinegar
Red wine vinegar
Sherry vinegar, preferably Spanish

CUPBOARD STAPLES
Anchovies, flat
Apricots, dried
Arborio, basmati, and jasmine rice
Arrowroot
Beef broth
Black turtle beans
Bulgur
Cannellini beans
Chicken broth, low sodium
Clam broth
Clams, chopped
Cornstarch
Crystallized ginger
Currants
Italian plum tomatoes
Jalapeño peppers, bottled
Long-grain white rice, not converted
Orange plums, dried
Orzo
Pinto or kidney beans
Polenta, instant Italian, imported
Porcini mushrooms, dried
Potato starch

Preserved ginger
Raisins
Tomatoes, preferably Muir Glen: diced,
 Fire-Roasted, sauce, and whole
Tomato paste, tube
V8 juice

SPECIALTY FOODS
Asian chili sauce
Asian fish sauce (*nam pla* or *nuoc mam*)
Asian sriracha sauce (Thai or Viet-
 namese)
Chinese five-spice powder
Chinese hoisin sauce
Chipotle peppers in adobo sauce
Hot dried chilies, small
Rice wine vinegar
Soy sauce, light and dark
Spanish smoked paprika, Pimentón de
 la Vera Extremadura—sweet, bitter,
 or hot
Toasted sesame oil
Unsweetened coconut milk, Thai

FROZEN FOOD
Baby lima beans
Corn, white
Green beans
Orange juice concentrate
Petite peas

SPIRITS
Angostura bitters
Dry red wine
Dry white wine
Madeira
Myers's dark rum

DOT COM SHOPPING

The ability to shop on the Internet for specialty items not readily available in supermarkets is a tremendous boon for the good cook. Here are a few Internet sites worth checking out:

beanbag.com: an intriguing selection of heirloom freshly dried beans

chiliaddict.com: flame roasted fresh and dried New Mexico chilies and other Southwest ingredients

earthy.com: professional chef's site for wild and exotic mushrooms, truffles, grains, oils, and vinegars, Asian food, edible flowers, ramps, baby veggies, and more

ethnicgrocer.com: around-the-world food shopping and all the gourmet basics

kalustyans.com: NYC's Indian specialty food store since 1944—now international ethnic foods

kingarthur.com: the premier baker's catalog

tienda.com: fine food and cookware, other products from Spain

zingermans.com: Ann Arbor's traditional Jewish deli and bakery on-line

SOUPS

1

S oup is the ideal make-ahead, put-away meal, or beginning of one. It's relaxing to make, comforting to eat, and keeps well either refrigerated or frozen. If you have good soup on hand, you can present a fast family supper with a composed salad and crusty bread or, often, by just adding bits of cooked meat, poultry, or seafood for substance. Nothing makes an easier or more impressive first course for dinner guests than homemade soup.

I prefer storing stock and soup in widemouthed glass jars because they save labeling and freeze perfectly—that is, if you remember to leave expansion room. I plucked a lot of broken glass from my freezer door before catching on. When freezing cream soup, you can avoid possible separation by freezing the base and whisking in the cream after it's thawed. Dense cream soups with a base like winter squash or potato, with small amounts of cream or milk, freeze and reheat just fine.

It's worth repeating that making your own stocks will help make you a better cook. The difference between homemade and canned stock is definitely measurable. Not that those cans of broth shouldn't sit front and center on your pantry shelf for times when intense flavors dominate or the freezer door is empty, but they shouldn't be your first choice. Making stock is so simple, and you can enjoy its sweet aroma while pummeling herbs into a meat loaf, baking a batch of muffins, or sorting your socks. Although skimming, straining, degreasing, and reducing can be a bit tedious, the compensation is in knowing exactly what went into that nutritious, delicious, endlessly useful elixir.

I use chicken and vegetable broth most often, and whether I reach for it from the cupboard or freezer depends on its flavor value to the dish. I don't reach for a can of broth when I'm making egg drop soup, nor do I waste my freezer stash on a spicy pork *rioja* sauce. For pure pleasure both in the preparation and the eating, I occasionally succumb to making beef or duck broth. The former is surprisingly expensive for bare bones and leathery meat that the butchers used to give away, but the latter is totally free when I ask to "ducky bag" the carcass after dining at my local Chinese restaurant.

A deep caramel-colored beef broth that turns to solid (or softly undulating) gelatin when chilled overnight can fill you with a crazy sense of virtue and a maniacal desire to hoard. There's something Flinstonian about roasting huge animal knucklebones and slabs of meat to render one's supper. Even without the classic clarifying raft of ground beef and egg white, the whole procedure suggests primitive appetites.

As for duck broth, it's sweeter and more elegantly complex than chicken. It's ideal for Asian soups.

All the recipes in this chapter benefit nutritionally from the use of homemade broth, but where its flavor isn't imperative, I have indicated that canned broth is acceptable.

Personally, I'm very fond of cold soups and feel they are underappreciated. The word itself may conjure up a steaming bowl of wholesomeness, but it's hard to beat the refreshing, sprightly taste of a chilled soup.

CHICKEN BROTH

Makes 2 quarts

*M*ost recipes for chicken broth call for using a whole, uncooked chicken or its parts. For years I've done that, but I'm not convinced you get substantially more flavor than you do from the carcass alone, particularly if it's been oven- or spit-roasted and hasn't been picked down to bare bones. My habit is to save bones in my freezer so I can make chicken broth when the mood strikes and time permits. You can increase the depth of flavor and the gelatinous quality of the broth by tossing in some uncooked wings, but that isn't as imperative as starting off with the carcass of a natural, unfrozen chicken. I don't mean it must be pricey or even free-range, just antibiotic-free, minimally processed, and naturally fed as opposed to those unseemly faux-birds. Even the big supermarkets now offer only marginally more expensive, natural birds.

I also have a hard time tossing all that chicken meat out after an hour or so of rendering its broth, but it's tasteless and, I'm convinced, nutritionally bereft. However, there is one way this works—see the technique for poaching chicken on page 51. If you do this, save the liquid and use it instead of water for making a super-rich and delicious broth with both the cooked bones and any carcasses you may have stored. Now we're talking real chicken broth! And there will be enough to get you through several recipes.

I also tend to use the maximum amount of vegetables because I like the flavor. If you have only one carrot, one celery stalk, or half an onion, just make less broth.

1 roast or rotisserie chicken carcass, not picked clean, including leg and wing bones

2 pounds wings or other chicken parts, or a second carcass waiting in the freezer

1 medium onion, peeled and quartered

2 small carrots, scraped and chopped

2 celery stalks, snapped in half

3 garlic cloves, peeled and smashed

1 bay leaf

3 fat sprigs of thyme and several stems of flat-leaf parsley tied together

2 teaspoons kosher salt

1/2 teaspoon whole black peppercorns

〜 Break up the carcass into small sections, removing any skin or visible fat. Place all the ingredients in a large stockpot and barely cover the contents with water. Bring to a simmer—not a boil—over medium-high heat. Cover and reduce the heat to low to keep the stock slowly simmering with small bubbles gently breaking the surface. Keep the lid ajar. Cook the broth for 2 hours, skimming the surface of foam with a wide, shallow spoon. Taste the broth and adjust the salt, if necessary. If the seasoning is right but it still tastes weak or watery, simmer for another hour. Beyond 3 hours, you can't hope to extract more flavor. As chickens differ in depth of flavor, so do broths.

Allow the broth to cool slightly before lifting out the bones and vegetables with a slotted spoon or a scoop sieve. (I drop them into a small garbage bag in the sink, where they can cool completely before being thrown out.)

Here's where a long-handled flat sieve does yeoman service, straining out every last peppercorn and snippet of debris. Otherwise, you can strain your stock through a fine sieve or a few layers of cheesecloth. At this point, if you want a more intense flavor or prefer storing a smaller quantity and adding water back in later, reduce the stock by one third to one half over medium-high heat.

Pour the broth into widemouthed freezer-proof glass jars and refrigerate overnight. Lift off any congealed fat from the surface, screw on the lid, and freeze for later use, or store in the refrigerator for up to a week. If you're still not ready to use it, bring the broth back to a full boil for 5 minutes and refrigerate again. Repeat as necessary.

COOK'S NOTES: *If you can remember, it's always smart to put away a couple of half-pint jars of broth for use in sauces.*

If you have a gas range without a simmer burner, it's helpful to use a heat diffuser to assure a steady low flame.

If you plan to use your broth for Asian soups, leave out the thyme and bay leaf and toss in 3 to 4 quarter-size slices of fresh ginger and a split stalk of trimmed lemongrass. Szechuan peppercorns are an interesting alternative to black.

BEEF BROTH

Makes 2 quarts

*F*rench onion soup would be unthinkable without a rich beef broth, and so would country American vegetable soup or Italian minestrone. When I worked in Rome, I survived on late-night suppers of restorative beef broth with a poached egg floating on top and heavily dusted with Parmigiano-Reggiano. It made me purr—audibly.

Besides soup, to have small quantities of reduced beef broth in the freezer for an impromptu sauce is that rare investment paying huge dividends.

Unless you're striving for consommé, don't worry if your broth isn't as clear as topaz. The clarity will improve if you bring the broth to a rolling boil for just a couple of minutes, adding the vegetables and seasonings as you reduce the heat. More often I simply toss everything into the pot at once and pray for full flavor. Regularly skimming any foam that forms on top is important, and I can't overemphasize that the best results come from preroasting the ingredients.

5 pounds all-beef or beef plus veal bones; knuckles, veal neck with meat, beef shin or shank	4 large garlic cloves, peeled and smashed
1 large onion, peeled and quartered	1 to 2 cups water
3 carrots, trimmed, washed, and cut in thirds (no need to peel)	1 bay leaf
	3 fat sprigs of thyme and several stems of flat-leaf parsley, tied together
3 heavy celery stalks, snapped in half, any strings pulled off	½ teaspoon whole black peppercorns
	2 teaspoons kosher salt

❧ Preheat the oven to 400°. Place the meat, vegetables, and garlic in a large roasting pan and roast for 45 minutes. Transfer the caramelized bones and vegetables to a stockpot. Pour off only the clear fat and place the pan over two medium-heat burners. Add 1 or 2 cups of water to the pan, scraping the bottom with a wooden spoon to release all the browned bits. Pour the dark brown liquid into the stockpot, barely cover the contents with water, and bring to a boil.

Add the remaining ingredients and reduce the heat until small bubbles gently break the surface, using a flame tamer over gas burners. Regularly skim any surface foam. Slowly simmer the broth, uncovered, for 4 hours, tasting to determine when it reaches a full, rich flavor. Adjust the salt, if necessary.

Remove the large solids with tongs. If you have a long-handled flat sieve, rake through the broth to capture stray bits and pieces. Otherwise, strain the broth into a saucepan through triple cheesecloth or a regular fine sieve. At this point the broth is ready to be reduced, if you choose to do so, or pour it into two 1-quart widemouthed glass jars. Store, uncovered, in the refrigerator until any remaining fat forms a solid coating on the surface. Lift the fat off with a teaspoon. Screw on the lid and freeze for later use, or store in the refrigerator for up to a week. If you're still not ready to use it, bring the broth back to a full boil for 5 minutes and refrigerate again. Repeat as necessary.

COOK'S NOTES: *To reduce the broth, let it simmer, uncovered, until it reaches the desired level of reduction. Take note of the original line of demarcation inside the pan to help determine how far you've gone with the reduction.*

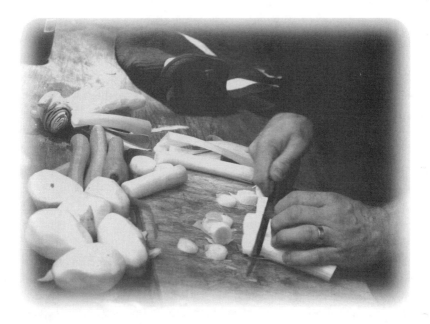

VEGETABLE BROTH

Makes 1½ quarts

Y ou'll need to make this only once to appreciate its ease and value. Using a vegetable broth base can highlight the flavor of hot or cold vegetable soups that don't necessarily require the enrichment of meat or poultry broth. This is particularly true of cold soup, where a fresh sparkle is often the key to success.

Buying leeks, carrots, and celery in bunches usually means there are leftovers languishing in the refrigerator and, if you're using this book, you'll have lots of garlic around. So all you need is fresh thyme, parsley, and a tomato. Vegetable broth is essentially court bouillon without the wine. If you want to poach fish, you can use your stored vegetable broth by simmering 2 cups of it with 1 cup of white wine. Not classic, but it works just fine.

2 leeks, trimmed, washed, and chopped

1 small onion, peeled and quartered

3 medium carrots, trimmed and cut in chunks (no need to peel)

2 heavy celery stalks with some leaves, if possible

1 plum tomato, seeded

4 whole garlic cloves, peeled

1 bay leaf

¼ teaspoon whole black peppercorns

2 sprigs of thyme tied together with several sprigs of flat-leaf parsley

2 teaspoons kosher salt

1½ quarts water

ℂ Place all the ingredients in a stockpot, bring to a boil, reduce the heat to its lowest point, and simmer the broth, covered, for 1½ hours. Taste for salt adjustment, if necessary. Allow the broth to cool before straining. If it isn't flavorful enough, return it to a simmer and reduce the broth by one-third.

COOK'S NOTES: *If you have stray herbs in your refrigerator that you would like to use up, add them to the broth in the last half hour. Tarragon or mint works well in limited quantity and so does basil, but hold the rosemary.*

When I'm in a high-speed mode and there's no veggie broth in my freezer, I often turn to the V8 juice in my cupboard, if my dish can handle the preponderance of tomato. An interesting aside: I'm told V8 was one of the late, great Chef Jean-Louis Palladin's favorite American products.

CREAM of MESCLUN SOUP

Serves 4 to 6

This is a surprisingly complex and perfectly delicious soup worthy of preceding a dinner party or, because it's so quick and simple to prepare, a special treat for the family. The addition of slivered ham and croutons transforms it to a satisfying main dish soup.

This soup is just as wonderful cold as it is hot, and either way, it packs a nutritional wallop. It has become a personal favorite of mine because I always seem to have an odd assortment of greens hanging around that never quite made it to the salad bowl. Proportions and individual quantities are unimportant as long as you have at least 3 packed cups of greens.

4 tablespoons (½ stick) butter

3 garlic cloves, minced

1¼ cups chopped sweet white onions or shallots

3 tablespoons minced flat-leaf parsley

2 tablespoons minced fresh tarragon or 1 teaspoon dried

1 bunch of watercress, heavy stems removed

2 cups tightly packed mesclun, including some baby spinach

1 quart Beef Broth (page 6) or Chicken Broth (page 4), homemade or canned

2 egg yolks

1 cup light cream or half and half

½ teaspoon kosher salt

Freshly ground black pepper

Pinch of cayenne pepper

Melt the butter in a Dutch oven. Add the garlic, onions, parsley, and tarragon and sauté over medium heat until the onion is translucent. Add the greens, reduce the heat, and stir well to combine. Pour in the broth and simmer, uncovered, for 15 minutes or until the greens are thoroughly wilted and soft. Whisk the egg yolks into the cream, add the seasonings, and pour the mixture into the soup. Continue whisking until the soup is slightly thickened. Remove from the heat and allow it to cool for a minute or two before pureeing in the blender or food processor. Reheat to serve.

You can safely store this soup in the refrigerator for 3 to 4 days. If you want to freeze it, puree the soup first, and whisk in the egg-and-cream liaison just before serving.

GARLICKY ROASTED FRESH TOMATO SOUP

Makes 5 cups

How bad is canned tomato soup? you might ask. Not bad at all. I always kept a nostalgic can of cream of tomato soup in my cupboard until I upgraded to tomato bisque, assuming fewer apologies would be necessary if I were ever caught can-handed. Seriously, canned soup is for the solo grilled cheese sandwich. Homemade soup is a special treat.

When every rural road is lined with summer farm stands, and smart supermarkets bring in local tomatoes, even tomato addicts like me run out of things to do with them. How many BLTs can one endure? Admittedly lots, but this is the time to squeeze some of that luscious ripe tomato taste into freezer jars for winter's dearth. And you can't beat cold tomato soups in the dog days of summer, either. Here's a simple base that can appear in many guises—each as delicious as the next.

2 pounds ripe tomatoes
Kosher salt and freshly ground black
    pepper
Sugar
Olive oil
1 quart homemade Vegetable Broth
    (page 8)

2 teaspoons tomato paste
1 tablespoon Roasted Garlic (page 155)
One 5½-ounce can low-sodium V8 juice
Minced parsley and basil, grated
    lemon zest, and toasted croutons
    for garnish

Preheat the oven to 225°.

Core the tomatoes and cut them crosswise. If you're using plum tomatoes, cut them lengthwise. Flick out the seeds and their juice with the tip of your finger or a knife. Lay them out side by side, cut side up, on a foil-lined sheet pan, or use a nonstick silicone liner. Sprinkle the tomatoes with salt and pepper and a few grains of sugar and brush, or spray, a little olive oil around the cut edges to keep them from burning. Roast the tomatoes 4 to 6 hours, or until most of the juice has been evaporated and they are dry enough to pick up. Remove them from the oven and set aside to cool.

The skin should pull off easily, but if some sticks to the edges, don't worry. Drop the tomatoes and any pan juices into a blender along with a couple of cups of the broth. Puree the mixture until it's very smooth and you can see only tiny flecks of skin and seeds. Pass the mixture through a food mill. If you have the time and patience, you can work it through a fine-mesh sieve.

Pour the strained soup back into the blender and add the tomato paste, garlic, and V8. Blend well and add the remaining broth. Taste for seasoning. At this point you can freeze the base for future use in soups or sauces. It will also keep in the refrigerator for several days. When you're ready to serve, hot or cold, garnish as suggested or use any one of the following:

a spoonful of corn kernels or Tomatillo and Green Chili Salsa (page 138)
a dollop of yogurt or sour cream swirled in
small cooked shrimp or lump crabmeat and diced avocado
grated Cheddar cheese or melted cheese toast

COOK'S NOTES: *This versatile soup can quickly be converted to a respectable gazpacho. For 4 servings, blend in 2 slices of day-old French bread, crusts removed, 1 rounded tablespoon of mayonnaise, and a splash of red wine vinegar to taste. Adjust the consistency if needed. Add diced, peeled, and seeded cucumber, diced red onion, and green pepper in any combination or quantity that suits your palate.*

CRAB and EGG DROP SOUP

Serves 4

The only way to make egg drop soup even better is to add crabmeat. You could, of course, gild the lily still further by adding slivered shiitake mushrooms and/or snow peas.

Any which way, you'll be glad you have homemade chicken broth or duck broth on hand, because a cup of this soup—followed by a spicy beef stir-fry or a roast chicken with Thai curry paste rubbed under the skin—makes a sensational start to a dinner party or family meal.

6 cups homemade Chicken Broth
  (page 4) or duck broth
2 garlic cloves, smashed
1 stalk lemongrass, trimmed, peeled,
  and split (optional)
3 quarter-size slices of ginger, minced
Salt to taste

1 tablespoon cornstarch mixed with
  2 tablespoons broth or water
2 eggs, lightly beaten
$^3/_4$ cup lump or back-fin crabmeat
2 scallions with $1^1/_2$ inches of green,
  minced

Bring the broth to a simmer and add the garlic, lemongrass, and ginger. Allow these to steep over low heat until the broth reaches the intensity of flavor you prefer. Strain the broth and check for salt.

At this point, you could cool and refreeze, or refrigerate for use later in the week.

To finish: Return the soup to a boil and stir in the cornstarch slurry until the soup thickens slightly and becomes clear. Slowly drizzle in the beaten eggs and stir once with a chopstick or the handle of a wooden spoon. Immediately remove from the heat and add the crabmeat. Garnish the soup with the scallions.

COOK'S NOTES: *If you want to add slivered shiitakes and/or snow peas, add them to the broth before finishing the soup. They will freeze in the broth perfectly well.*

A lovely alternative for this converted Asian-style broth is to simmer it with several handfuls of stemmed baby spinach and a dozen thawed frozen shomai, *available now in most supermarkets; just delete the eggs and optional snow peas.*

SEAFOOD CHOWDER

Serves 4

This is probably my favorite way to eat seafood. I can have most of my favorites in one bowl, and it's far less fussy than a proper Mediterranean bouillabaisse, which never seems to translate well. This is not a recipe to be frozen when finished, but it can be successfully made in stages and, even after the fish is cooked, it can be stored for 3 to 4 days. Like the other soups in this chapter, the base itself can be frozen, which makes the completion of the soup a snap. Don't let the long list of ingredients deter you—this is a very simple soup to prepare.

You can vary the seafood and vegetable ingredients any way you like, and the quantities themselves are just as forgiving. As with many soups, you can safely play around with the recipe and make it your own.

One 5-pound bag of farmed mussels
2 shallots, minced
1/2 cup dry white wine
2 garlic cloves, smashed
3 tablespoons butter
1/2 medium onion, chopped
1 fresh red chili, ribbed, seeded, and
  minced
Kosher salt and freshly ground
  pepper
2 cups clam broth
One 14-ounce can low-sodium chicken
  broth
2 tablespoons flour, plus 1 tablespoon, if
  desired
1 cup 2 percent milk
1 cup corn kernels, fresh or frozen
1 cup peeled, diced potatoes
2 cups lightly packed julienned Swiss
  chard or beet greens
1/3 pound each shrimp, cod, and bay
  scallops
1/2 cup heavy or light cream
4 strips smoked bacon, cooked and
  crumbled
Minced parsley or cilantro for garnish

Rinse the mussels under running water and put them in a stockpot with the shallots, wine, and garlic. With the lid on, turn the heat to medium-high. In 3 to 5 minutes the shells should open. Pull the mussels out with tongs to a colander, tipping them so the juice runs back into the pot. Leave any closed shells behind, replace the lid, and steam for another minute or two. If any of the mussels still don't open, discard them. As soon as they're cool enough to handle, remove the open mussels to a bowl, discarding the shells. Carefully pour the mussel broth into a cup, leaving any sediment or grit in the bottom of the pot. Rinse the pot in hot water and put it back on the stove.

Melt the butter and sauté the onion and chili in the stockpot until both are soft and the onion is translucent. Salt and pepper to taste. Whisk in the 2 tablespoons flour and cook briefly while heating the clam and chicken broth in a small saucepan. Slowly add the hot broth to the roux, whisking constantly until the mixture is smooth and thickened. Add the milk and stir over medium heat until the soup base lightly coats the back of the spoon. If you prefer a thicker soup, pour a little hot base into an additional tablespoon of flour and whisk until smooth. Stir it back into the soup base. Bear in mind that the starch in the potatoes will also thicken the soup.

At this point, the base can be cooled and frozen or refrigerated for finishing another day.

To finish: Thaw the corn if frozen. Steam the diced potatoes with the Swiss chard and corn in a small amount of water in the microwave for 2 to 3 minutes on high, until the potatoes can be pierced easily with the tip of a knife. Drain.

Peel and devein the shrimp, if necessary, and cut the cod into bite-size chunks. Bring the soup base to a simmer and add 1½ cups of the mussels along with all the other ingredients except the bacon and the herb garnish. The soup will be ready to serve as soon as the shrimp turn pink and the fish is translucent. Sprinkle the herbs and bacon over the top.

COOK'S NOTES: *Refrigerate the leftover mussels for another use. Try reheating them in Lemon-Chive Sauce (page 143) or the Creamy Garlic Sauce (page 141) and serve over a grilled chicken breast. Or add them chilled to a green salad with a splash of sherry vinaigrette.*

GRILLED ASPARAGUS SOUP
with SHIITAKE MUSHROOMS

Serves 4

W*e can now treat asparagus to the magical alchemy of caramelization.* The asparagus in this recipe are broiled and not grilled, but the effect is quite similar. If you happen to be grilling one day, by all means toss some asparagus on the fire and save them for making soup another day.

Although asparagus says spring to me, it's now available year-round and, particularly in the less flavorful winter months, it's a treat to be able to make this marvelous soup.

The only negative that comes to mind when I think of asparagus is that it tastes infinitely better peeled. Many will groan in disbelief, I know, but I accepted the fact years ago and now I simply whip out the peeler and get on with it.

So many soups require a touch of cream to marry the ingredients, and this one is no exception. If you can't tolerate even this minimal amount, you could leave it out. In that case, the appearance will be more pleasing if you don't blend it. Instead, cut the asparagus in 1-inch pieces, add them to the broth along with the mushrooms, and omit the spinach.

1 pound asparagus, thick ends snapped off, lightly peeled down from the tip
3 tablespoons butter
4 shallots, peeled and thinly sliced
8 to 10 baby spinach leaves, slivered
Kosher salt and freshly ground black pepper
1/2 teaspoon Beau Monde seasoning
Pinch of cayenne pepper
11/2 quarts homemade Chicken Broth (page 4)
11/2 cups stemmed shiitake mushrooms, slivered
1/2 cup half and half or light cream, or 1/3 cup heavy cream
Grated Parmigiano-Reggiano

Pour a little neutral oil in your cupped palm and rub your hands together. Now run your fingers through the asparagus to coat them very lightly, especially the tips. Spread out the spears single file on a broiler pan, tip to tip. The toaster oven works fine. Broil them on the middle rack, rolling them over once, until a knife pierces the thick end easily. To avoid burning the fragile tips, protect them with a thin strip of foil after you roll them over. (You want the stalks to pick up toasty golden brown spots.) Remove the asparagus to a paper towel and blot. Cut off one half of the tips for garnish. Set aside.

Melt 1 tablespoon of the butter in a sauté pan and add the shallots and the spinach leaves. Salt and pepper and sprinkle with the Beau Monde and cayenne. Sauté over medium heat until the shallots are soft and the spinach thoroughly wilted. Remove to a paper towel, blot, and place in a blender. Add a couple of cups of broth and process to combine. Cut the asparagus spears in sections and add to the blender. Puree until very smooth. Pour the soup into a large pitcher or bowl along with the rest of the broth and the cream, and stir to blend.

At this point, you can refrigerate or freeze the base to finish another day. If you have prepared the asparagus tips and mushrooms, store them in a sealed plastic bag in the fridge or freeze until you're ready to use them.

To finish: Melt the remaining butter in a sauté pan and quickly stir-fry the shiitake slivers. Salt and pepper lightly. Stir the mushrooms and asparagus tips into the hot soup and serve with grated Parmigiano-Reggiano.

COOK'S NOTES: *If you have Caramelized Onions (page 126) in the fridge, you can make an interesting variation on this soup by blending them with the asparagus and broth and swirling in fromage blanc or crème fraîche when you're ready to serve. (Both are now readily available in most well-stocked supermarkets). Omit the mushrooms.*

FRIED CORN and TOMATO CHOWDER with SHRIMP

Serves 4

Leftover corn on the cob is the best way to be reminded of this ideal summer supper soup, although I've made it successfully in the winter with frozen white corn. The zesty flavor makes it a star in any season.

2 cups sweet corn, cut off the cob, or frozen white corn, thawed and blotted dry
$\frac{1}{2}$ teaspoon sugar, if necessary
3 strips lean smoked bacon
1 medium onion, chopped
2 garlic cloves, smashed and minced
Kosher salt and freshly ground black pepper
$\frac{1}{2}$ to 1 red jalapeño pepper, seeded and deveined

1 tablespoon minced fresh oregano or 2 teaspoons dried
$\frac{1}{2}$ cup heavy cream
1 quart Vegetable Broth (page 8) or Chicken Broth (page 4), homemade or canned
$1\frac{1}{2}$ cups diced tomatoes, fresh, or one $14\frac{1}{2}$-ounce can, preferably Muir Glen
Squeeze of lime
1 cup cooked shrimp, chopped
$\frac{1}{4}$ cup minced flat-leaf parsley
3 tablespoons minced cilantro

Fry the corn in a dry nonstick skillet over medium-high heat until it starts to crackle and picks up brown flecks. If the cob corn is not really fresh, dust it with a half a teaspoon of sugar. Set the corn aside.

Fry the bacon until crisp, drain it on a paper towel, and crumble or cut it into small bits. Set aside. Pour off all but a tablespoon of the fat and add the onion, garlic, salt, pepper, and the chili. Sauté until the onion is soft and translucent. Scrape the mixture into the blender along with half the fried corn, the cream, and about a cup of the broth. Puree until smooth.

At this point, the soup can be either refrigerated or frozen for later use.

When you're ready to heat and serve, combine the base with the remaining corn and the rest of the ingredients, reserving the cilantro and bacon bits for garnish.

PUMPKIN-PEAR SOUP

Serves 4

The next time you see an orange mountain of those perky little sugar pumpkins, don't think tabletop jack-o'-lanterns—think soup. Make sure you're buying edible, not field, pumpkins. They not only make great soup but, hollowed out, they're both attractive and thermal soup or stew containers. Remember to save the lids!

This is a lovely, satisfying soup that need not be prepared just with pumpkin. Any winter squash, like butternut, will do nicely.

1 small pumpkin or small round winter squash
2 Bosc pears, peeled, cored, and quartered
2 tablespoons butter
1 medium sweet onion, diced
2 garlic cloves, smashed and minced
4 quarter-size slices of ginger, slivered
1 teaspoon garam masala
1/2 teaspoon ground cumin

1/8 teaspoon cinnamon
1/4 teaspoon cayenne pepper
1 teaspoon kosher salt
2 tablespoons frozen orange juice concentrate
1 tablespoon lemon juice
3 cups Chicken Broth (page 4), homemade or low-sodium canned
1/3 cup heavy or light cream

Preheat the oven to 375°. Cut the pumpkin in half, or cut off the top if you're using it as a bowl. Scrape out the seeds and bake cut side down until tender, about 30 minutes. Spoon off any stringy pulp and set aside 1 cup of the soft flesh, saving the rest for another use.

Cook the pears in some of the broth in the microwave on high for 3 to 5 minutes, until soft. Set aside.

Melt the butter in a skillet. Sauté the onion, garlic, and ginger over medium-high heat until the onion is soft. Lower the heat, add the seasonings, and stir to combine. Cook for a minute or two to release the flavors. Add the pumpkin or squash, the orange juice concentrate, and the lemon juice. Scrape the contents of the skillet into the blender along with the pears and enough of the broth to make a smooth emulsion. Puree, and then add the mixture to the rest of the broth; add the cream and whisk to blend. Taste for seasoning.

The finished soup freezes well.

CHICKEN MULLIGATAWNY

Serves 4

There are so many versions of this aromatic Anglo-Indian soup that it's difficult to discern which among them is authentic, and I dare to add my own over-the-top version to the chaos. I prefer using coconut milk in lieu of cream to soothe and enrich the spicy ingredients. Although lamb, or no meat at all, is a faithful choice, I think chicken results in a more elegant soup.

Mulligatawny is a lot of fun to make when you have the leisure to enjoy cooking with these rarely used spices that fill the air with their delectable, exotic aroma. In spite of the lengthy list of ingredients, this is a simple project that takes very little time to complete.

If you don't have cooked chicken on hand or a plump fresh one to quick-poach (see page 51), make the soup base and store it as suggested below.

4 tablespoons (½ stick) butter
1 medium onion, diced
2 garlic cloves, minced
1 to 2 small red chilies, seeded and
    minced
2 teaspoons grated gingerroot
1 teaspoon ground cumin
1 teaspoon turmeric
2 teaspoons ground coriander
1 teaspoon garam masala
1 teaspoon kosher salt
2 tablespoons flour
1½ tablespoons lime juice

2 teaspoons sugar
2 tablespoons ketchup
One 14-ounce can unsweetened light
    coconut milk
1 tablespoon cornstarch mixed with
    2 tablespoons broth (optional)
1 quart Chicken Broth (page 4), prefer-
    ably homemade, or low-sodium
    canned
4 cups cooked, boned chicken, pulled
    into chunks
⅓ cup minced cilantro for garnish

∾ Melt the butter in a skillet and add the onion, garlic, chili(es), and gingerroot. Sauté until the onion is soft and translucent. Add the spices and cook over low heat for a couple of minutes to release their flavor. Whisk in the flour until the mixture is smooth. Whisk in the lime juice, sugar, and ketchup. Add the coconut milk and simmer over low heat until the mixture thickens slightly.

At this point, the base can be cooled and stored in the refrigerator or freezer to be used at a later date.

To finish: Heat the broth and add to the soup base. If you prefer the soup thicker, make a slurry of 1 tablespoon of cornstarch and 2 tablespoons of the broth and stir in. When the soup is smooth and creamy, add the chicken, heat it through, and garnish with the cilantro.

BEEF and VEGETABLE SOUP

Serves 4 to 6

T*his is the all-American vegetable soup of my childhood.* It was always served with hot cloverleaf dinner rolls, and I could never resist tapping their plump rising tops.

If you don't have Beef Broth on hand and you want to start the day by making some, add two or three meaty short ribs to it, removing them after the first hour and a half when they should be tender enough to shred into the finished soup.

However, if you have the broth and want some visible meat in the soup, either braise the ribs separately for this purpose, sliver some leftovers, or pull a few small meatballs from your freezer to add at the end.

2 quarts homemade Beef Broth
   (page 6); not canned
1½ cups finely shredded green cabbage
½ cup peeled and diced young carrots
1 cup frozen baby lima beans
⅔ cup corn kernels, fresh or frozen

1 cup cut string beans, fresh or frozen
1 cup canned plum tomatoes, stemmed
   and shredded, with their juice
1 cup shredded beef (optional)
Kosher salt and freshly ground black
   pepper

Bring the broth to a simmer in a large stockpot. Add the cabbage and carrots and cook until tender. Add the remaining ingredients and continue simmering over medium-low heat until all the vegetables are soft. This is not grown-up soup with al dente vegetables.

Serve with crusty bakery bread or cheese biscuits.

COOK'S NOTES: *Needless to say, you can make adjustments or substitutions to this recipe. In place of the meat, try chickpeas, Great Northern beans, or a small soup pasta like orzo or pastene. I like it best almost as thick as a vegetable stew, but you can certainly thin it by reducing the amount of vegetables or by adding a cup or two of water if your broth is intense enough.*

BLACK BEAN SOUP CUBANO

Serves 8 to 10

There's no point in making only four servings of a soup that freezes so perfectly. Besides, if you're going to soak and cook dried beans, you might as well use the whole package, right?

There's differing opinion on soaking beans. I prefer soaking them because I never know how old the beans are, and by soaking them overnight you can be assured they won't take longer to cook than you planned. Black beans are particularly stubborn that way.

I've reworked this soup so many times I'm no longer sure whether it's more Cuban or Puerto Rican. What I can assure you is that it's a very tasty and soul-satisfying main dish.

1 pound dried black beans, soaked
    4 hours or overnight
1 bay leaf
4 garlic cloves, peeled and left whole
1 small onion, stuck with 2 cloves
1 quart Beef Broth (page 6) or Chicken
    Broth (page 4), homemade or canned
1 tablespoon kosher salt

The Sofrito:
1/4 pound lean salt pork, diced
Olive oil (optional)
1 jalapeño pepper, seeded and minced
    (optional)
1 medium onion, diced

4 garlic cloves, smashed and minced
1 small green bell pepper, seeded and
    diced
1/2 teaspoon ground cumin
1/2 teaspoon dried oregano
1 cup drained plum tomatoes, chopped
1/2 cup slivered smoked ham
Kosher salt and freshly ground black
    pepper

Assembly:
2/3 cup rum or Madeira
4 hard-boiled eggs, chopped, for garnish
1/4 cup minced cilantro for garnish

☙ Drain the beans and put them in a stockpot with the bay leaf, garlic, onion, and broth. Bring quickly to a boil and turn the heat down to its lowest level. Cover and simmer the beans until tender, hopefully about 1½ hours. Check for doneness after an hour and add salt. Check regularly after that, adding water if they become dry.

Meanwhile, make the sofrito. Render the salt pork until the meat is crisp and there's enough fat left in the pan to sauté the rest of the ingredients. If there isn't enough, add a little olive oil. The jalapeño is not a traditional sofrito ingredient, but I think a bit of heat complements this soup. If you agree, be sure to taste the chili before adding it. Some are hot—some are not. Sauté the onion, garlic, and chili until the onion is soft and translucent. Add the rest of the sofrito ingredients and simmer for a minute or two.

When the beans are soft, fish out the bay leaf, garlic, and onion and taste for salt. Stir in the sofrito and taste again. Adjust the seasoning and consistency; if you want the soup thinner, add more broth or water.

This is a good point to store or freeze the soup for later use. The flavor will improve if it's stored for a day or two before serving.

To finish: Add the rum to the base and bring the soup to a gentle simmer until steaming hot. Garnish with the chopped eggs and cilantro.

COOK'S NOTES: *Lime juice or red wine vinegar, which you can choose to replace the rum or Madeira, are frequent additions to a Latin black bean soup. Two tablespoons of sherry vinegar would also be a good option.*

MIXED MUSHROOM SOUP with LEEKS

How fortunate we are to have such abundance of exotic fresh mushrooms in our markets today. They may not be wild, as in gathered-in-baskets-by-fair-maidens in the forest, but there's hardly a familiar variety we can't buy now. This must be very hard on our loyal standby, the little white button. Whatever we can't find fresh we can surely find dried, and a combination of both makes intensely flavorful soup.

This is yet another ideal do-ahead recipe because the herbed mushroom base will store for several days in the refrigerator, or it freezes very well. It can either be used to complete this soup or to make a sauce for meat or fish.

Although I'm very fond of creamed mushroom soup, I'm offering this version creamless, which is not to say that you couldn't swirl a tablespoon of heavy cream into each serving or even float a small dollop of crème fraîche on top.

A word about the seeming extravagance of exotic mushrooms. When it comes to chanterelles, morels, lobster, oyster, shiitake, or other sticker-shock varieties, remember that mushrooms are very lightweight and you need only a small amount in the mix to gain the complexity of flavor you want. For the required amount of mushrooms, I would buy a pound of cremini and/or baby portobellos (a teenage cremini) and make up the half-pound with the pricier options.

The hazelnut garnish is a Joyce Goldstein touch, which I find brilliantly complementary.

$\frac{1}{2}$ ounce dried mushrooms, porcini or
   any kind

4 tablespoons ($\frac{1}{2}$ stick) butter

1 large or 2 small leeks, trimmed and
   chopped, white part only

2 garlic cloves, smashed and minced

1 teaspoon fresh thyme leaves

3 sage leaves, julienned

Light grating of fresh nutmeg

$1\frac{1}{2}$ pounds mixed fresh mushrooms,
   wiped clean and trimmed as
   necessary

Canola oil

Kosher salt and freshly ground black
   pepper

2 to 3 tablespoons dry sherry or
   Madeira

2 quarts beef or chicken broth

1 tablespoon arrowroot or cornstarch mixed with 2 tablespoons
   water

Toasted chopped hazelnuts and minced
   flat-leaf parsley for garnish

Barely cover the dried mushrooms with hot water and allow them to reconstitute for only 20 to 30 minutes. Drain them into a cup or mug, reserving the liquid and allowing any grit or sediment to sink to the bottom. Mince the mushrooms and set aside.

Melt the butter in a stockpot and add the leeks, garlic, and seasonings. Sauté over medium heat until the leeks are soft and remove from the pan, leaving as much butter as possible behind.

Try to cut the mushrooms in keeping with their shape. Buttons should be cut in halves or quarters, and odd shapes should be cut so their identity is still discernible. Add a little canola oil to the remaining butter, raise the heat, and toss in the dried and fresh mushrooms. Sauté, tossing often, until they shrink and pick up flecks of golden brown. Return the leeks and seasonings to the pan and salt and pepper the mixture. Taste the mixture and adjust the seasoning if necessary.

At this point, the soup base can be refrigerated or frozen for later use, either in this soup or as a base for meat, poultry, fish, or pasta sauce.

To serve, put the base in a soup pot and add the sherry or Madeira, allowing it to sizzle a second. Pour in the broth and bring to a simmer over medium heat. Taste. Thicken the soup with the arrowroot or cornstarch slurry. It takes a couple of minutes. Serve the soup with the suggested garnishes.

If you choose to add a dollop of crème fraîche or sour cream, sprinkle the top of it with the nuts and parsley.

BABY SPINACH SOUP with COCONUT MILK

Serves 4

This soup has those Asian flavors I crave, and it's equally delicious hot or cold. I discovered that while foraging in the fridge one afternoon and sipping a little straight from the glass jar. What a splendid beginning to a Thai chicken salad! (See box, page 52.) If you have the spinach, it can be made spur of the moment and enjoyed immediately—or successfully refrigerated or frozen. It's quite elegant enough to serve guests.

1 tablespoon canola oil

1/4 teaspoon toasted sesame oil
   (optional)

3 garlic cloves, smashed and chopped

2 quarter-size slices of ginger, slivered

1/4 cup chopped shallots

Kosher salt and freshly ground black
   pepper

Grated zest of 1 lime

2 teaspoons brown sugar, not packed

1 quart homemade Chicken Broth
   (page 4) or Vegetable Broth (page 8)

1 pound prewashed baby spinach,
   stemmed

One 14-ounce can unsweetened light
   coconut milk

1/2 teaspoon Thai or Vietnamese
   sriracha or other hot chili sauce
   (available in Asian or specialty food
   stores)

Heat the oils in a soup pot and sauté the garlic, ginger, and shallots until the shallots are soft. Add salt and pepper. Add the lime zest and brown sugar and stir to combine.

Add the broth and spinach and bring to a boil. Reduce the heat and simmer for 5 minutes. Cool slightly and transfer to the blender. Puree until the mixture is smooth. Add the coconut milk and sriracha sauce and pulse to blend.

Heat and serve or store in the refrigerator or freezer.

CHILLED ROASTED BEET and CUCUMBER SOUP with DILL

Makes 2 quarts

This may be the best chilled soup I've ever devised, and it's a visual knockout besides. Non–beet lovers are converted and everyone raves. What further reward is there for so little effort?

4 large beets or 6 of mixed size

1 large cucumber, peeled, seeded, and diced

2 cups homemade Vegetable Broth (page 8)

1/2 cup sour cream (low fat is fine)

1/2 cup yogurt (low fat is fine)

1 teaspoon kosher salt and freshly ground black pepper

2 teaspoons hot honey mustard

2 tablespoons raspberry or rice wine vinegar

2 tablespoons minced fresh dill

Additional dill and sour cream for garnish

⌇ Preheat the oven, or toaster oven, to 350°. Cut the stems off the beets to within an inch of the top but do not clip the root. Put the unpeeled beets on the middle rack and roast for an hour or more, or until the skin is somewhat crispy and the beets have obviously shrunk inside their skins. They should now be well caramelized. Put them aside until cool enough to handle and then slip them out of their skins, working over the sink. Cover your cutting board with a sheet of wax paper so it won't be stained, and roughly chop the beets. Measure out a cup and a half and slide them into the blender. Store any extra beets in the refrigerator, dressed with balsamic vinegar. It's a great cook's treat.

Add the cucumber to the blender with the broth and puree until very smooth. Pulse in the rest of the ingredients except the garnish and taste to adjust the seasoning.

Chill thoroughly and serve with a puff of sour cream sprinkled with dill.

CHILLED TURKISH TOMATO SOUP

Serves 4

This was one of the more popular cold soups served in my former restaurant and one that I often ordered myself when I went downstairs to the dining room for a cup of soup and a quick cheese omelet. Why we called it Turkish I really can't recall.

1 tablespoon olive oil
4 scallions, trimmed and chopped
1/2 teaspoon Curry Powder (page 123)
Pinch of thyme
1 tablespoon chopped mint leaves
Kosher salt and freshly ground black
    pepper
3 cups Garlicky Roasted Tomato Soup
    (page 10), or 1 1/2 cups V8 juice,
    1 1/2 cups tomato juice, and 1 table-
    spoon Roasted Garlic (page 155)

2 to 3 dashes Tabasco
2 tablespoons lemon juice
Grated zest of 1/2 lemon
Pinch of sugar
1 cup yogurt
Julienned basil leaves or minced
    flat-leaf parsley for garnish

Heat the olive oil in a small sauté pan and add the scallions, curry powder, thyme, mint leaves, salt, and pepper. Stir over medium heat just until the scallions soften and the spices release their aroma. Scrape into a blender and add the tomato base, Tabasco, lemon juice, zest, and sugar. Puree until very smooth. Add the yogurt and pulse to thoroughly combine. Taste for seasoning.

Refrigerate the soup for several hours before serving with the garnish of julienned basil.

FROSTY MINTED SWEET PEA and CUCUMBER SOUP

Serves 4 to 6

*J*ust the name of this soup wipes the dew from your brow. Mint, peas, and cucumber are as soothing a combination on a steamy summer day as the lazy breeze from a ceiling fan on the veranda.

1 pound frozen baby peas
1½ cups homemade Chicken Broth
   (page 4)
½ large cucumber, peeled, seeded, and
   chopped
¼ cup chopped scallions, white part
   only

Kosher salt and pepper, preferably
   white pepper
¼ cup chopped chives
½ cup chopped mint leaves
Pinch of cayenne pepper
1 cup yogurt
½ cup half and half or light cream

Puree all but the yogurt and half and half until the mixture is very smooth. Taste for seasoning and strain through a fine sieve, pushing the solids through with the back of a wooden spoon. Whisk in the yogurt and cream. Chill several hours before serving.

COOK'S NOTES: *Only the little sweet peas—baby peas—can be used for this soup. The larger, more starchy peas will dull the fresh taste. If fresh English peas are in the market or at your local farm stand and you enjoy shelling them, as I do, by all means buy a couple of pounds. I always buy even more because I'm one of those "shell a few, eat a few" raw pea lovers.*

THE AMAZING BRAISE

2

There's little better than a juicy flash-fried chop or a crispy grilled fish, but too often they appear on the table long before the creativity of cooking can kick in. In the interest of time, we've become a nation of short-order cooks, stuck in the quicker-is-better mode. After dumbing down the culinary process awhile, one's interest in it must wane. Just ask any mother whose children develop lockjaw at the sight of anything green and beg for orange cheese—with a face printed on it.

Slow cooking involves different techniques in a single dish and offers a good opportunity to hone your culinary skills. It also provides a chance to improve your kitchen efficiency by making you aware of wasted motion, disorganized storage, equipment chaos, and pantry shortages. Using your kitchen fully—its tools, your hands, your experience, talent, curiosity, and the sensitivity of your palate—is what will make cooking fascinating for a lifetime.

There is little difference between stewing and braising—the former traditionally involves more liquid than the latter. A stew usually simmers lingeringly on top of the stove, uncovered, while braises cook in a slow oven, tightly lidded. Most of the recipes in this chapter represent my arranged marriage of the two techniques. More often than not, I prefer oven braising without a lid because it preserves the careful browning of the meat, and the dish leaves the oven with an appealing intense glaze. The exception is chicken parts, especially when it includes the breast meat. With or without the bones, it needs less time to cook and can be done more successfully on top of the stove.

Braising and stewing can teach a great deal about the properties of their ingredients, and most beg experimentation since the origin of their recipes is often dubious. Crossing ethnic boundaries can completely change the character of a dish from one country to the other regardless of faithful recording. Different cuts of meat differ widely in texture and flavor—and everyday chickens aren't what they used to be. Our tomatoes don't thrive in the same soil as those of southern Italy, and a pepper isn't just a pepper no matter where it grows. There are no absolutes for something as subjective as flavor. You start with the declared success of someone else's invention and eventually let your own palate rule, preferring a little more of this, less of that. What I find amazing about the multi-ingredient dish is the complexity of flavor you can build into it or, conversely, how it can be reduced to its essential purity.

There are no fish or seafood recipes in this chapter. They simply don't store or reheat well. You will, however, find many complementary, make-ahead accessories for fish in the Condiments, Salsas, and Sauces chapter.

The recipes here are a mere hint of the many slow-cook dishes you can prepare in stages, or finish and store. Also, they can all be doubled in quantity and frozen for weeks later when you're ready to enjoy them again.

If you really get into this, you might consider investing in a home vacuum sealer. This is great for lengthy freezing without fear of crystallization or freezer burn. One caveat: The package shrink-wraps to the precise configuration of its contents, so trying to stack varying shapes of frozen lumps on a shelf is a Lucy sight gag. Until I bought a storage basket, a shower of food-rocks landed on my foot each time I opened the freezer.

BEEF BRAISED in SPICED RED WINE

Serves 6

This is a sophisticated braised-beef-for-all-seasons. Leftovers can be quickly adapted to a sauce for fettuccine or ricotta-filled ravioli.

2 tablespoons olive oil

2 tablespoons minced pancetta or slab bacon

2 pounds beef chuck, well trimmed, cut in 2-inch cubes

Kosher salt and freshly ground black pepper

Grated nutmeg

4 garlic cloves, smashed and minced

$1/2$ medium onion, thinly sliced

4 whole cloves and one 1-inch piece of cinnamon stick, tied together in cheesecloth

1 cup dry red wine

2 large ripe tomatoes, peeled and chopped, or canned Italian plum tomatoes with their juice

2 cups sliced fennel

$1/4$ cup minced flat-leaf parsley

Grated lemon zest for garnish

✺ Preheat the oven to 350°, positioning a rack in the middle.

Heat the olive oil in a shallow Dutch oven or deep ovenproof sauté pan over medium-high heat. When it's hot enough to sizzle, add the pancetta and sauté until crisp. Remove from the pan and reserve. Sauté the meat in the remaining fat until well browned on all sides. (This may have to be done in batches to prevent crowding the meat.) Add salt and pepper. Remove the meat from the pan and dust very lightly with grated nutmeg.

Add the garlic and onion and sauté until the onion is limp. Add back the pancetta and meat cubes along with the cheesecloth sack, wine, and tomatoes. Adjust the level of the liquid to just below the top of the meat. Slide the pan, uncovered, into the oven and braise for 2½ to 3 hours or until the meat is fork-tender. Check on the liquid level every so often, while turning the meat over into the seasoned mixture. About an hour before it's done, add the fennel. Taste and lightly salt and pepper again, if needed. Add the parsley.

Remove the meat and fennel from the sauce. Discard the seasoning sack. Over medium-high heat, reduce the sauce to a thickness that will generously coat the meat and then return the meat and fennel to the sauce. Lightly garnish with grated lemon zest and serve with cannellini puree (page 106).

COOK'S NOTES: *If you want to make this dish in two stages, follow the recipe until after the meat has braised for a couple of hours. Cool and refrigerate or freeze the beef. Add the fennel to finish the dish.*

SPICY TEQUILA CHUCK

Serves 4

Tequila, like sake, has an intriguing flavor. Neither is comparable to another. A small amount can elevate a dish from plain to distinctive. This recipe is a good example of that and, with the popularity of margaritas, you're bound to have some tequila in your liquor cabinet; I think gold tequila is best.

I marked my test notes for this recipe with a very unprofessional "yummy."

¼ cup canola or olive oil

4 thick strips of beef chuck, about
    2 x 2 x 6 inches

Kosher salt and pepper

1 large onion, chopped

4 garlic cloves, chopped

1 hot red chili, seeded and slivered

3 celery stalks, chopped

1 teaspoon pure chili powder

¼ teaspoon cinnamon

¼ teaspoon ground cumin

¼ cup tequila

1 large ripe tomato, peeled, seeded,
    and chopped or 1 cup canned plum
    tomatoes with some of the juice

1½ cups Beef Broth (page 6) or
    Vegetable Broth (page 8), homemade
    or canned

¼ cup minced cilantro for garnish

∾ Preheat the oven to 350°.

Heat the oil in a shallow Dutch oven or a deep ovenproof sauté pan over medium-high heat until shimmering, and brown the meat well on all sides. Add salt and pepper. Remove the meat and reserve. Pour off all but a couple of tablespoons of the oil and sauté the onion, garlic, chili, and celery until the mixture is soft. Stir in the chili powder, cinnamon, and cumin. Pour in the tequila and simmer the mixture for a couple of seconds to evaporate the alcohol and release the flavors of the spices. Add the tomato and broth and nestle the meat into the pan. (The level of liquid should not reach the top of the meat.) Slide the pan, uncovered, into the oven and braise the meat for 2 to 3 hours or until it is fork-tender. Check the broth level after 1½ hours to judge how rapidly the meat is cooking.

Remove the meat from the sauce and slice it thickly. Reduce the sauce if needed. Return the meat to the sauce and serve with the cilantro garnish.

COOK'S NOTES: *This dish can be fully completed and refrigerated or frozen.*

For most of us, chili powder is an easy shop from the supermarket spice rack. It has the familiar flavor we associate with chili con carne, but since it contains complementary ingredients like cumin it isn't pure chili powder. Look for Vanns Spices or try specialty food stores for the pure powder, or check the online sources in the front of the book.

SHORT RIBS BRAISED with THREE-COLOR PEPPERS

Serves 6

*O*f all the options for selecting which cut of beef to braise, I think short ribs are the best. They have the most intense beef flavor and enough marbling to deliver the unctuous result you expect from slow-cooked meat. Leaner cuts may seem a more prudent choice, but you end up adding fat to help break down the fibers from the outside, and the finely textured meat still tastes dry.

Slow-cooked short ribs, with their bare bones hanging out, have a rather unattractive appearance, and many people are fastidious about dealing with them on their plates. My solution is to make these succulent ribs more user-friendly by laying them on my cutting board and performing a little basic surgery. First I cut off the bone and, with a very sharp utility knife, remove the tough band of gristle that runs beneath it. Then I remove any plugs of clinging fat from the meat that might be eaten accidentally or confiscated by the fat police. Finally, I cut the meat into thick slices and return them to the sauce, making certain to pour the vagrant juices back into the pan. Messy, but generous of spirit.

If you're not going to serve the ribs that night, you could go to the next step and refrigerate the sauce and meat separately. That way you can also scrape off any solidified fat on the surface of the sauce.

¼ cup canola or olive oil
6 meaty center-cut beef short ribs
Kosher salt and cracked black pepper
2 teaspoons hot Spanish smoked paprika (*pimentón*) or hot Hungarian paprika
1 large onion, chopped
6 garlic cloves, smashed and chopped

3 bell peppers: 1 each red, yellow, and orange, stemmed, seeded, and cut in strips
1 large tomato, peeled, seeded, and chopped
1 cup V8 juice
1 cup Beef Broth (page 6), homemade or double-strength canned
Minced flat-leaf parsley for garnish

➤ Preheat the oven to 350°.

Heat the oil in a shallow Dutch oven or deep ovenproof sauté pan over medium-high heat until it shimmers, and brown the ribs well on all sides. Remove them from the pan and season with the salt, pepper, and paprika. Pour off all but a couple of tablespoons of the remaining oil and sauté the onion and garlic until the onion is soft. Add the peppers, tossing to wilt them slightly. If the pan becomes dry, drizzle in a little more oil. Add the tomato and combine.

Nestle the ribs into the mixture and pour in the V8 and broth, adjusting the liquid to a little below the top of the meat. Slide the pan, uncovered, into the oven and braise for 2 to 3 hours. Check the liquid level every so often and redistribute the contents of the pan.

Test the meat after 2 hours and every 30 minutes thereafter. When the ribs are ready, the bones will be totally exposed and the meat fork-tender. (Don't be tempted to remove them before or the results will be disappointing.)

If the sauce needs reduction, remove the meat with tongs to the cutting board and spoon the peppers into a bowl. Reduce the remaining liquid over high heat and be sure to taste for seasoning before you reassemble the dish. Garnish with the parsley just before serving.

COOK'S NOTES: *If you want to prepare this dish in stages, braise the ribs as instructed without the peppers. Remove the bones, trim the meat as suggested in the headnote, and refrigerate or freeze. When you're ready to serve the dish, sauté the peppers until soft and add them to the sauced meat. Simmer until hot and garnish with parsley.*

LAMB SHANKS with DRIED APRICOTS

Serves 6

*L*amb shanks are not the rock stars of the meat case* in spite of their bizarre appearance. They do project a certain homey charm, however, and prove that it's really what's inside that counts. Young lamb from the United States and the lamb from Australia and New Zealand take the lamb shank out of the category of rank mutton, which may be one reason for the renewed interest in this very succulent cut of meat.

The flavor of lamb fat, no matter how young, turns me off, so I spend a little time trimming all visible fat from the shanks, including the skin that surrounds it. All you need is a sharp knife and some patience.

Lamb shanks take as well to intense seasonings as they do to fruit, and this recipe uses both. Here's a chance to try out those Preserved Lemons you made.

4 pounds lamb shanks, trimmed
3 tablespoons olive oil
1 red onion, chopped
6 garlic cloves, smashed and chopped
1/2 teaspoon ground ginger
1/2 teaspoon ground allspice
1/2 teaspoon ground cumin
1/4 teaspoon turmeric
1/8 teaspoon cayenne pepper, or to taste
1/4 cup brandy or cognac
Pinch of Spanish saffron threads or two
    .125-gm packs of powdered saffron

2 cups Beef Broth (page 6), preferably
    homemade
1 cup water
12 dried apricots, cut in thirds
1/4 Preserved Lemon (page 125), rind
    only, diced, or a few threads of grated
    lemon zest
One 2-inch piece of cinnamon stick
Fat bunch of flat-leaf parsley and
    cilantro, tied together with a long
    string for retrieval
2 teaspoons to 1 tablespoon honey

☙ Preheat the oven to 350°.

Using a Dutch oven or lidded ovenproof sauté pan over medium-high heat, heat the oil until it shimmers and brown the lamb well on all sides. Remove the shanks and pour off all but a couple of tablespoons of the oil.

Sauté the onion and garlic until soft. Add the dry spices and stir to combine. Add the brandy and allow it to simmer for a minute to evaporate the alcohol. Crush the saffron threads into the mixture and add the broth with the remaining ingredients, except the honey. Taste for seasoning and add the honey by the teaspoonful to achieve a pleasing balance. (Remember that the apricots will disintegrate and add their own hint of sweetness, so it's wise to hold back on the full amount of honey until the end.) Return the meat to the pan.

Unlike the other braises in this chapter, I use a lid to cook the shanks, because their surface now has no protective fat or skin. Either way, it will take about 3 hours before the meat truly falls off the bone.

Remove the tied herbs and serve with minted bulgur or couscous.

COOK'S NOTES: *As in the recipe for short ribs, my preference is to remove the shanks to the cutting board and release the meat in large chunks before returning it to the sauce. In so doing, you can pull out the quite obvious tendons that are unpleasant to chew and difficult for diners to extract.*

LAMB with FAVA BEANS AVGOLEMONO

Serves 6

*L*amb, dill, and lemon are as Greek as a cheeseburger and pickles are American. I can't speak for the fava beans except that they have never gained the popularity here that they have in Europe. They're perfectly wonderful and I have seen them recently in grocery stores, not only fresh but frozen and canned. When you see the long twisted pods in the market, try remembering this dish, because fresh is best. Peeling them is a surreal experience; Mother Nature protected the precious bean the way an oyster protects a pearl.

2 tablespoons olive oil
1 tablespoon butter
2 pounds lamb shoulder, cut in cubes
1 medium onion, finely chopped
Kosher salt and freshly ground black
    pepper
1 cup Chicken Broth (page 4), preferably
    homemade
3 tablespoons minced fresh dill

2 cups shelled fava beans, fresh or
    thawed frozen

Avgolemono Sauce:
2 eggs, beaten until pale in color
Pinch of salt
3 tablespoons lemon juice
1 cup boiling chicken broth

 Heat the oil and butter in a shallow Dutch oven or a deep sauté pan. Sear the lamb, in batches if necessary, until it's brown on all sides. Add the onion, salt, pepper, and the broth. Cover the pan and braise on top of the stove or in a preheated 350° oven for 1½ to 2 hours until the meat is fork-tender.

Add the dill and fava beans and simmer for 15 minutes or until the beans are tender. Canned will take less time.

To make the sauce, combine the beaten eggs with the salt and lemon juice. Off the heat, slowly whisk in the boiling broth. When the sauce thickens, add it to the hot meat and beans and serve.

COOK'S NOTES: *To make this dish in stages, braise the meat and store or freeze. Cook the fava beans separately and store. When you're ready to serve, add the dill and the beans and prepare the Avgolemono Sauce. Stir the sauce into the hot meat, but do not let the sauce come to a boil or it will curdle.*

TRINIDAD CURRIED PORK

Serves 4 to 6

Although the island of Trinidad has a relatively large population of immigrant East Indians, this curry definitely evidences its Caribbean influence. It's a wonderful, spicy concoction redolent of the cuisine of the tropics.

2 tablespoons butter

2 tablespoons canola oil

2 pounds pork butt, cubed and lightly
   dusted with flour

1 medium onion, chopped

4 garlic cloves, smashed and chopped

1/2 teaspoon kosher salt

1 1/2 teaspoons Curry Powder (page 123)
   or store-bought curry with
   1/2 teaspoon garam masala

1/2 cup dark rum, preferably Myers's

1 cup Beef Broth (page 6), homemade or
   canned

3/4 cup unsweetened coconut milk

1 1/2 tablespoons honey

Cayenne pepper to taste, if needed

1 tablespoon arrowroot or cornstarch, if
   needed

1/2 cup slivered almonds, toasted, for
   garnish

 Heat the butter and oil in a shallow Dutch oven or deep sauté pan. Brown the meat cubes on all sides, in batches if necessary. Remove and set aside. Drain off the excess fat, leaving a couple of tablespoons and all of the browned bits. Add the onion, garlic, and salt and sauté over moderate heat until the onions are limp but not brown. Add the curry powder. Stir to combine and sauté a minute to release the full flavor of the spice. Pour in the rum and let it sizzle to evaporate the alcohol. Add the broth, coconut milk, and honey. Simmer for 1 minute and taste. Add the cayenne if the mixture needs more heat.

Return the pork to the sauce. Cover the pan and simmer over low heat for 30 minutes. Remove the cover and simmer for 30 minutes more or until the meat is fork-tender. The coconut milk and the flour bits from the browned meat should thicken the sauce sufficiently to cling to the meat. If not, make a slurry with the arrowroot and a little water and whisk it into the sauce. Garnish with the slivered almonds and serve.

Serve with rice and Asian Pear and Mango Chutney (page 135).

COOK'S NOTES: *This curry tastes better the second or third day and freezes very well.*

VEAL RAGOUT

Serves 6

I *made this one night for friends,* accompanied by their lanky teenage son who generally eats like a picky bird. So, when he asked for more, I knew it belonged in this book. I almost called it Dave's Ragout, but that made it sound like a diner's special, and this is a sophisticated, gently seasoned dish with a velvet mouth-feel fancied by young adults whose palates are not yet jaded. Pearl onions are a nuisance to peel but they contribute greatly to the flavor and presentation. They seem to be available year-round now in little net bags. If you can't find them, use frozen pearl onions and save yourself the peeling.

1 ounce dried mushrooms, any kind or mixed

2 tablespoons canola oil

2 tablespoons butter

2 pounds veal shoulder, cut in cubes

Kosher salt and freshly ground black pepper

1 cup dry white wine

1 cup homemade Chicken Broth (page 4)

24 white pearl onions, 10 ounces, peeled

3 thin young carrots or baby carrots, cut on the diagonal

2 teaspoons tarragon leaves, minced

2 tablespoons potato starch mixed with 2 tablespoons water

¼ to ⅓ cup heavy cream

Pinch of cayenne pepper (optional)

Soak the mushrooms in hot water to cover for 20 minutes. Strain and reserve the liquid.

Heat the oil and butter in a shallow Dutch oven or deep sauté pan. Add the veal and brown well on all sides. Add salt and pepper. Add the reconstituted mushrooms. Pour in the wine, broth, and the reserved mushroom liquid and bring to a simmer. Cover the pan and cook over low heat until the meat is fork-tender, about 45 to 60 minutes.

After 20 minutes, add the onions, carrots, and tarragon. Salt and pepper again, lightly, if required.

When the meat and vegetables are tender, remove the cover, add the potato starch slurry, and after the sauce thickens slightly, add the cream and cayenne. Taste for seasoning. Simmer for a few minutes to allow the cream to further thicken the sauce.

COOK'S NOTES: *You can cook this dish in two or three stages. Braise the meat first and store or freeze. When you're ready to serve, complete the dish. Or, finish the preparation through cooking the onions and carrots, and add the thickening and cream just before you serve.*

OSSO BUCCO PICCANTE

Serves 4

*V*eal shanks make a superb dinner any time of the year, and if there are any leftovers—or if you plan leftovers—the chopped veal makes a lovely pasta sauce. I'm sure there's no rationale to my sense that the marrow inside that little bone is wildly healthy, but, no matter; it lends a sumptuous quality to the lean and tender veal.

2 tablespoons olive oil

1 tablespoon butter

4 veal shanks

Kosher salt and freshly ground black pepper

¼ cup balsamic vinegar

2 garlic cloves, smashed and minced

¼ teaspoon red pepper flakes

2 teaspoons fresh oregano, roughly chopped

2 cups chopped canned Italian plum tomatoes, with some of their juice

¼ cup chopped flat-leaf parsley

 Preheat the oven to 350°.

Heat the oil and butter in a shallow Dutch oven or deep ovenproof sauté pan. Add the shanks and brown them well on both sides. Add salt and pepper. Add the balsamic vinegar and allow it to sizzle while you turn the veal over into the glaze. Add the remaining ingredients and slide the pan into the oven, uncovered. Bake for 1 to 1½ hours or until the meat releases from the bone and is fork-tender. (Do not undercook or the dish will be disappointing.)

COOK'S NOTES: *If you store this ragout for later use, cover the pan and reheat the veal gently in the sauce. Do not let the sauce boil or the veal may toughen.*

AEGEAN CHICKEN

Serves 4

I have a serious weakness for red, and not quite red, peppers. Perhaps it's because red peppers were considered so exotic when I opened my restaurant in 1972 that I had to special-order them from California.

This simple dish has the flavor and aroma I associate with the Greek Islands, and it looks good enough to take center stage for spur-of-the-moment guests.

It will keep several days in the refrigerator and will reheat well, but I don't recommend freezing it.

3 bell peppers: 1 each red, yellow, and
    orange
1/4 cup olive oil, plus more for drizzling
6 chicken thighs, rinsed and patted dry
Kosher salt and freshly ground black
    pepper
1 red onion, sliced
3 garlic cloves, smashed and minced
3 potatoes, peeled and thickly sliced
    (Yukon Golds are perfect)
1 tablespoon minced mint leaves

1 tablespoon chopped oregano leaves
1/4 Preserved Lemon (page 125),
    pulp removed and rind diced
    (optional)
1/2 bottle dry white wine
One to two 14-ounce cans low-sodium
    chicken broth
12 Kalamata olives, pitted and halved
1/3 cup crumbled feta cheese, preferably
    Bulgarian

❧ Roast the peppers (see Cook's Notes, page 45) until the skins are thoroughly charred, and put them in a paper or plastic bag until they're cool enough to peel. Cut off the stem end, slit the peppers lengthwise along their natural indentations, and remove the seeds along with any white interior ribs. Set aside.

Preheat the oven to 350°.

Heat the 1/4 cup of olive oil in a shallow Dutch oven or large ovenproof sauté pan until it shimmers. Sprinkle the chicken with the salt and pepper and sear it over medium-high heat until deep golden brown and crispy, about 12 to 15 minutes. Set the chicken on a plate and pour off all but a tablespoon or two of the oil from the pan. Add the onion and garlic and sauté until the mixture is soft but not browned. Layer the potato slices over the mixture and then the fresh herbs and preserved lemon. Replace the chicken. Arrange the peppers between and over the chicken pieces. Pour in the wine and broth until it reaches two-thirds of the way up the side of the pan. Slide the pan, uncovered, into the oven and bake for about an hour or until the chicken has pulled away from the bones.

The potatoes will soak up a lot of the broth, so check the liquid level and add more when and if you think it necessary. This is a good time to taste the braising liquid for seasoning, adjusting if necessary. You do want to end up with a juicy, moist dish, but you don't want a lot of broth sloshing around that you have to pour off or reduce.

When the chicken is done, sprinkle the top with the Kalamata olives and feta cheese. Drizzle a little olive oil over the top and run the pan under the broiler just long enough for the cheese to pick up a golden hue.

COOK'S NOTES: *I roast peppers on my gas range over a 10-inch round grate with primitive little wooden knob handles. I've seen these no-name gadgets advertised in catalogs selling Mexican or Southwestern food and cookware. You can also pierce the pepper's stem end with a long-handled fork and twist it directly over the flame or electric burner until black. That's all right if you have only one pepper to roast, but when there are multiples, slide them under a preheated broiler about 3 inches from the flame or element and watch them closely. If you try to blacken every crevice, it's easy to see them collapse from their internal steam and lose all texture. Frankly, if two-thirds of the skin is blackened, the rest should loosen enough in the bag to peel easily.*

CHICKEN with SPICY SAUSAGE, OKRA, and TOMATOES

Serves 4

*C*hicken and sausage are a welcome couple, but—okra? It's one of the few wallflowers of the produce stand, maybe not as homely as celeriac but even more misunderstood. Leave it whole, sauté it, steam it, or boil it and it will reward you with its nutritional deliciousness and by keeping its "goo" to itself. Buy okra only when it's fresh, young, and bright green and never when it's mature and bruised. It shouldn't be hard to remember that, like the rest of us, it only bleeds when you cut it.

This is a braise that doesn't benefit from long, slow oven cooking, so using your choice of chicken parts works well here, and cooking it on top of the stove is simpler.

3 tablespoons canola oil, plus more if needed

1/2 pound small fresh okra or frozen pods

1/2 pound spicy pork or chicken sausage

Dredging mixture of 1/2 cup masa (or all-purpose flour and cornmeal), 1/2 teaspoon ground cumin, and 1 teaspoon chili powder

Kosher salt and freshly ground black pepper

6 to 8 boned chicken parts, rinsed and blotted dry

2 garlic cloves, smashed and minced

1 medium onion, sliced

1 cup dry red wine

One 14 1/2-ounce can diced tomatoes, preferably Muir Glen

1 cup tomato sauce

꿈 Over medium-high heat, cook the oil in a large sauté pan or shallow Dutch oven until it is shimmering. Trim the stems of the okra down to the crown but do not cut into the pod. Turn the heat down to medium and sauté the okra for about 10 minutes. Remove and reserve.

Slice the sausage thickly and sauté in the oil remaining in the pan until browned. Remove and reserve. Do not discard the oil.

Spoon the masa (corn flour) or part all-purpose flour and part cornmeal into a large plastic storage bag. Season with the ground cumin, the chili powder, salt, and freshly ground black pepper. (Don't fuss over quantities and proportions.) Shake the bag to combine and shake the chicken parts in it to dust them lightly but thoroughly.

Reheat the remaining oil and add more if needed to sear the chicken. When the oil is very hot, add the chicken parts and sauté until brown and crisp on both sides. Remove the chicken, season with salt and pepper, and reserve. Don't discard the oil in the pan.

Add the garlic and the onion to the hot pan and sauté until the onion is limp, being careful not to burn the garlic. Salt and pepper lightly. By now the oil will look a bit funky, but don't worry; it's infused with the essence of the dish and valuable. Add the red wine and let it sizzle for a second or two and then add the tomatoes and sauce. Stir to combine. Check the seasoning and adjust to your taste. Be fearless, this dish should have *chutzpah*.

Add back the sausage and chicken, nestling the pieces in a single layer. If they don't fit, use two sauté pans, or switch the contents to a covered oven casserole or a small roasting pan you can cover with foil.

Cover the pan(s), reduce the heat to low, and braise the chicken for 30 minutes. Stir in the okra and cook for another 15 minutes, or until the chicken releases easily from the bone.

COOK'S NOTES: *If you want to make this dish ahead, keep the okra separate and combine it with the chicken when you're ready to serve.*

CORNISH HENS ANGOSTURA

Serves 4

I really do like succulent little Cornish hens. They're sweet, moist, and tender, and now that larger birds are being produced, and half of one makes the ideal single serving, they look more appetizing and less intimidating on the dinner plate.

As for Angostura bitters, I have memories of my dad's bar where that curious little paper-wrapped bottle was tipped carefully over a sugar cube, which was crushed meticulously with a mulling stick to make what I'm certain was a perfect old-fashioned. My childhood fascination ended with the aroma of the bitters, which was strangely akin to mincemeat. The tiniest drop on the tongue explained its name.

I recently discovered that the back of the paper wrapper is packed with useless, but curiously romantic, information. Who knew that it was formulated by a Dr. Siegert in Angostura, Venezuela, in the early nineteenth century and that it was originally sold as a stomachic, anti-flatulent, and appetite stimulant before it made the incongruous leap from the chemist to the barkeep. Today the only authentic bitters is manufactured in Trinidad, by appointment from Her Majesty Queen Elizabeth II.

Incidentally, this is an elegant and delicious dish quite presentable enough for guests.

2 large Cornish hens

Seasoning Paste:
4 tablespoons (½ stick) soft butter
1 teaspoon paprika
1 teaspoon turmeric
¼ teaspoon cayenne pepper
1 tablespoon grated orange zest
Kosher salt and freshly ground black
    pepper

2 tablespoons butter
1 tablespoon canola oil

Braising Liquid:
1 tablespoon butter
3 walnut-size shallots, minced
¼ cup frozen orange juice concentrate
2 teaspoons Angostura bitters
1 teaspoon honey
Pinch of cayenne pepper
2 cups Chicken Broth (page 4), prefer-
    ably homemade

2 teaspoons arrowroot or cornstarch

❧ Cut off the wing tips with a poultry shears. Cut along both sides of the backbones and remove. Turn the birds skin side down and cut out the thick center of the breastbones and discard. Locate the wishbone just below the neck opening with your fingers and remove it with a sharp paring knife. Now only the tiny breastbones must be removed, and that can easily be done with a sharp knife. Turn the birds skin side up.

Combine the ingredients of the seasoning paste and smear it under the skin, pushing your finger under the leg skin to loosen it. Reach in with the paste as far as you can. To protect the breast meat from overcooking, fold up the hen under the leg so that the leg is on top and you have a neat, small package wrapped in skin. You can tie it, skewer it, or sew it into place, any way that's easiest for you. (Appearance doesn't matter since the ties will be released later.)

Preheat the oven to 350°.

Heat the butter and oil until very hot in a shallow Dutch oven or deep ovenproof sauté pan. Brown the partially boned hens well on both sides. (You may have to do them in batches.) If you have a large stove-top casserole that all four halves will fit into without crowding, use that.

Pour in the braising liquid until it's not quite to the top of the hens. Slide the pan, uncovered, into the oven and bake for 45 minutes to an hour. When the meat pulls away from the leg bone and their juice runs clear, they are done.

Remove the hens to a plate and taste the sauce for seasoning. Thicken it to your liking with a slurry of arrowroot or cornstarch mixed with some of the pan juices. Whisk to combine and simmer until it reaches the desired consistency. Return the hens to the pan to heat through.

Remove the strings or skewers and serve with a wild rice pilaf.

COOK'S NOTES: *This dish can be prepared ahead completely and, after being brought to room temperature, can be reheated briefly in a 325° oven.*

CHICKEN BRAISED with FENNEL and TOMATO

Serves 6

If you're a dark meat chicken fan, you'll love this braise as much as I do. You could use only thighs, but the whole leg makes an ideal single serving. Although not all-American, this is comfort food at its best.

You can serve this with your favorite side dish—or none at all—but I urge you to try it first with pureed cannellini (page 106), Great Northern, or borlotti beans. The soft, moist texture of the cannellini pairs particularly well with the fennel sauce. Fold the cooked beans into the sauce once it's reduced, or serve the beans separately.

6 whole chicken legs (drumsticks and
    thighs)
5 tablespoons olive oil
¼ cup capers, rinsed and dried
Kosher salt and cracked black pepper
4 garlic cloves, smashed and minced
2 carrots, trimmed and diced
2 leeks, trimmed, washed, and chopped
2 medium heads of fennel, trimmed
    and chopped, fronds reserved

¼ cup minced fennel fronds
1 teaspoon fennel seeds, ground or
    crushed
1½ teaspoons sugar
One 14½-ounce can tomatoes, prefer-
    ably Muir Glen Fire-Roasted
2 cups Chicken Broth (page 4), prefer-
    ably homemade

Preheat the oven to 350°. Remove any visible fat or excess skin around the chicken legs.

Heat 3 tablespoons of the oil in a shallow Dutch oven or large ovenproof sauté pan until shimmering. Fry the capers until crisp. Remove with a slotted spoon and set aside on a paper towel to drain.

Rinse the chicken and pat dry. Sprinkle both sides with salt and pepper and sauté in the remaining oil, skin side down first, over medium-high heat until they're deep golden brown and crispy, about 12 to 15 minutes. (A 12-inch sauté pan will hold only four whole legs, so sear the chicken in batches to brown it properly.) Set the legs aside on a plate and pour off the oil. Wipe out the pan with a paper towel and add the remaining 2 tablespoons of oil.

Add the garlic, carrots, and leeks and sauté over medium heat until softened. Return the chicken legs to the pan along with the rest of the ingredients, except the reserved capers, and braise in the oven, uncovered, for 1½ hours. If there still seems to be too much liquid, remove the chicken and vegetables, strain the sauce, and reduce it to the desired consistency. Reassemble the dish and garnish with the fried capers.

THE POACHED CHICKEN

*W*hat is this recipe doing here? It isn't close to a braise and it's the opposite of a slow-cook, but when I came across it scribbled on an aged note card I knew immediately it fit the time-out, do-ahead, multiuse kind of kitchen magic I wanted this book to illustrate. I revisited the technique, using ginger and lemongrass to season the broth for an Asian dinner party dish. I recalled that the Chinese use this method often, which is undoubtedly why I wrote it down back when I immersed myself in Chinese cooking.

Recently I caught a Jacques Pépin television program on which he started a French dish with this chicken and said that he got the idea years ago from his good friend Danny Kaye. If you're old enough to fondly remember who Mr. Kaye was, you might have known that in addition to his comic genius, he was considered one of the best nonprofessional, serious Chinese cooks in the country with an enviable wok station in his West Coast kitchen.

From the kitchens of China, Danny Kaye, Jacques Pépin, and me, here's a winner of a technique I'm certain you will try often.

1 quart Chicken Broth (page 4), homemade or low-sodium canned
One 3-pound fresh naturally fed chicken
1 leek, trimmed to 1 inch above the
   white part, split and washed
1 carrot, scraped and split lengthwise

1 celery stalk
1 small bunch of sprigs of parsley and
   thyme, tied together
Kosher salt and freshly ground black
   pepper

ᗅ Place all the ingredients in a stockpot and weigh them down with a small upside-down plate with a jar on top—or any other heatproof, sanitary way to keep the chicken from floating out of the broth.

Bring the broth to a boil, reduce the heat, and simmer for 20 minutes. Remove the pot from the burner, remove the weight, put a lid on the pot, and let it sit for 1 hour undisturbed, or you can leave it until the broth is cool. Amazingly, the bird will be perfectly cooked and deliciously moist. The skin and bones will fall from the carcass if you started with a fresh chicken, and you'll have a double-rich broth to refrigerate or freeze for other uses. Taste it before storing, should it need to be reduced for more intense flavor.

The breasts will come away from the bone in two solid pieces, as will large chunks from the thigh. Store the breasts and other large pieces separately from the small bits, since you'll probably find different uses for each.

COOK'S NOTES: *If you plan to use the chicken and/or the broth for Asian dishes, omit the parsley and thyme and substitute several sprigs of mint and/or basil, 6 quarter-size slices of ginger, 2 peeled garlic cloves, and 2 lemongrass stalks, trimmed and split.*

USE THE CHICKEN TO:

- Make your favorite chicken salad with the smaller pieces.

- Make a Thai chicken salad with minced garlic, hot chilies, grated ginger and lime zest, lots of minced scallions, slivered basil and mint, lime juice, peanut oil, rice vinegar, a pinch of sugar, salt, and pepper.

- Make a Quick Skillet Coconut Curry. Sauté minced onion, ginger, and garlic in peanut oil. Add Curry Powder (page 123) or Thai Green Curry Paste (page 124) to taste and pour in a 14-ounce can of unsweetened coconut milk. Simmer until thickened and add the chicken.

- Make the Chicken Mulligatawny soup (page 19). You're halfway there.

- Make an Asian-inspired soup. Simmer rice or noodles in the broth and add baby spinach, sautéed shiitakes, and chicken bits.

- Reheat the breasts in Tomatillo and Green Chili Salsa (page 138), thinned with a touch of cream.

- Make individual pot pies with a combination of sautéed leeks, whole shallots or red pearl onions, slivered smoky ham, and minced parsley. Bind with a sauce of reduced chicken broth, a splash of Madeira or port, and a cornstarch slurry to thicken. Top with lids of the Sour Cream Turnover Pastry you froze last week (page 177).

- Coat large pieces of room-temperature chicken with any Flavored Mayonnaise suggested on page 120. Serve on a bed of mixed greens.

- Smother the hot chicken with Caramelized Onions (page 126).

- Make Turkish Chicken Walnut. Remove the crusts from 2 slices of white bread and soak in 1/3 cup of chicken broth. Process to a paste 1 cup of walnut pieces, 2 garlic cloves, and the bread squeezed, but still moist. Slowly add another cup of broth until the mixture is thick and creamy. Cover the room temperature chicken with the sauce. Drizzle with a mixture of Hungarian paprika and olive oil.

- Make Spinach and Chicken Cannelloni. Mix 2 cups minced chicken with 1 cup ricotta, 2 pressed garlic cloves, 1 cup minced cooked spinach, blotted dry, 1/3 cup grated Parmigiano-Reggiano, 1 egg, beaten, grated nutmeg, pinch of cayenne pepper, salt, and pepper. Roll up in 4 x 6-inch strips of cooked lasagne sheets and bake with Tomato *Concassé* (page 142) or freeze for later use.

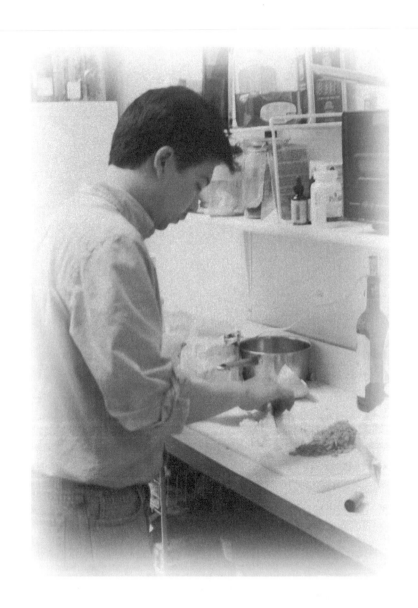

GROUND MEAT AND STUFFINGS

3

W hen we think of ground meat, meat loaf comes immediately to mind if not the iconic hamburger. Everyone loves a tasty juicy meat loaf but in spite of its many ethnic relatives and the efforts of some new millennium chefs to spin it onto the trendy culinary hit parade, it clings to its homey image.

A perfect meat loaf is no longer a given as, once again, too lean meat often wreaks havoc on the juicy factor. The addition of cream or an extra egg yolk boosts the moisture level and is more convenient than searching out and mixing in the pork fat of the ancestral French country terrine. The recipes in this chapter suggest ways of expanding your thinking beyond the all-American meat loaf, including how to dress it up for company.

As for meat loaf's plump round cousins, meatballs, they suffer in part from their unfortunate name. The mention of "balls of meat" leads more often to a grimace than a lick of anticipation. The Italian word *polpette* sounds much more appetizing. Some still insist that golf-ball-size meatballs belong on a wad of spaghetti, a combination unheard of in Italy, where they are always respectfully served alone. Tiny brandied lamb meatballs are popular in Spanish *tapas* bars, and ethereal steamed pork or shrimp balls are ubiquitous around the Pacific Rim. Authentic Swedish meatballs, with their gingersnap spices, are tricky to make but delicious. In brief, it's hard to find a country that doesn't have its own version of ground meat in a variety of shapes. At cocktail parties I've catered, unusual meatballs always disappear like cookies stolen from the jar.

Once you've been successful with meatball recipes you'll look forward to the creative pleasure of improvising with ground meat. You might even succumb to grinding your own to ensure freshness, control the fat content, and attain the best texture. Despite warnings of ending up with mousse, careful pulsing in the food processor does a fine job with no mess. A baked meat loaf in the refrigerator is a treasure. You can either reheat it or serve it cold. While you're working with ground meat, consider using part of the mixture to make and freeze meatballs, large or small.

Most meat loaves and meatballs benefit from reheating in a simple pan sauce to retain their moisture. Although I've included sauces where they're most appropriate, check out those listed in the Condiments, Salsas, and Sauces chapter. When time is short, a hefty slice of cold meat loaf on country bread toast, lavished with garlic mayonnaise and a slice of ripe tomato, makes a dandy supper.

I've included a quartet of recipes for croquettes in this chapter, hoping that some readers aren't afflicted with the fear of frying. For those who are, shallow-frying is a less bothersome option than deep-frying. If it's the oil you fear, and not the process, you can bake croquettes with very good results thanks to the availability of Japanese bread crumbs, *panko,* which mysteriously hold their crunch. The beauty and appeal of a croquette is the crispy shell that provides textural contrast to its soft interior.

Technically, a croquette is a blend of seasoned ground meat or seafood bound with a thick cream sauce, but even that caloric extravagance is avoidable. A vegetable puree like potato, broccoli, or cauliflower will do the trick and adds another flavor dimension to the contemporary croquette. Croquettes may seem dated to those of you who groaned over those gummy ones as dutiful children, but they're truly worthy of reincarnation.

Making sausage is a subject about which excellent books have been written. I'm making only a quick pass at preparing bulk sausage, yet it can be a guide to developing your own signature sausage. You can make small links and even a large *saucisson* by shaping and encasing your mixture in plastic wrap and poaching it in the microwave or in a pot of boiling water. No pig intestine casings to seek out or struggle with, and no special equipment is required. The sausage can be quickly browned in a sauté pan just before serving. The cooked *saucisson* can be chilled and sliced for the cheese board, picnic, or cold buffet with no casing to peel. Once you make your first successful bulk breakfast sausage, you might be inspired to experiment.

Making and storing stuffing of various kinds makes quick work of family meals and can turn ordinary vegetables and small birds into special presentations. The best vegetables to stuff are onions, tomatoes, squash, peppers, eggplant, and mushrooms—particularly the big bold portobello. A moist and piquant stuffing in a chicken or a Cornish hen can make an otherwise dull bird chirp. There are often leftover bits and pieces in the refrigerator that lend themselves to tasty stuffing combinations such as grains, bread, mushrooms, corn, nuts, cheese, ham, and herbs. Before tossing out that leftover chicken, add some grated cheese, corn, and rice and fill a couple of bell peppers ready to bake a couple of days later. Once again, having a few things from the Condiments, Salsas, and Sauces chapter on hand can give a grain or bread stuffing just the flavor boost it needs.

GROUND MEAT REMINDERS

1. If you buy meat already ground, it isn't safe to refrigerate it for more than 2 days. If you buy slab beef chuck, pork butt, and veal shoulder, you can refrigerate it longer—or freeze it, weighed and labeled—to grind or process yourself when you have time.

2. Ground meat mixtures can be frozen either raw or cooked and can be used interchangeably as meat loaves, meatballs, kebabs, and turnovers or to enhance the fillings of stuffed vegetables.

3. The meat and seasoning must be thoroughly combined but never compacted or overmixed, because the texture will be dense.

4. For optimum flavor, refrigerate any seasoned ground meat mixture for at least 8 hours, or overnight, before baking.

5. In my opinion, the only acceptable filler is day-old bread. If it must be soft sandwich bread, toast it before soaking it or it will simply dissolve and won't lighten the mixture. European-style bread with the crusts removed works best, but I've also had success with sliced whole grain bread.

6. The egg acts as a binder to prevent the meat from crumbling. Generally, one egg is sufficient for a pound and a half of meat or less. An added yolk enriches the meat, as does the addition of milk, cream, sour cream, or cheese.

7. A ground meat mixture ready for baking should feel wet and cohesive, not dry and crumbly.

8. Always cook and taste a small patty of meat so that you can adjust the seasoning and consistency. If it falls apart, add another egg. If it needs a flavor boost, add additional seasonings.

CHICKEN MEAT LOAF with HAM and RICOTTA CHEESE

Serves 4 to 6

This is a terrific, versatile meat loaf that bears no resemblance to its macho cousins. Its dainty size, pâté-like texture, and pale golden hue set it apart from the usual mashed potato and gravy crowd. Even though it makes a wonderful sandwich on whole grain bread with a slice of homemade Refrigerator Pickles (page 134), it's elegant enough to grace a buffet, hot or cold.

¼ pound smoked ham

1 pound ground chicken

½ pound ricotta cheese

⅓ cup grated Pecorino cheese

2 teaspoons puree Roasted Garlic
   (page 155)

2 eggs, beaten

Kosher salt and freshly ground black
   pepper

Grating of fresh nutmeg

Pinch of cayenne pepper

5 fresh bay leaves for garnish (optional)

Preheat the oven to 350°.

Pulse the ham in a food processor until it's fluffy. Put all the ingredients into a wide, shallow bowl, using a light hand with salt if the ham is salty. Use a fork to carefully combine the mixture completely. Since it's hard to identify the varying shades of white ingredients, diligent mixing is important. (The mixture will be quite wet.) Pour it into a loaf pan, press the bay leaves into the top decoratively, and bake for 1¼ hours. Allow the loaf to cool slightly before attempting to unmold it, or chill completely to serve cold.

This loaf keeps well in the refrigerator but is not a good one to freeze.

MEXICAN MEAT LOAF

Makes one 5 x 9-inch Loaf or one 5½ x 3-inch round, or several small meatballs

ere's a big robust meat loaf that reflects my love of Mexican food. It defies the usual 2-to-1 ratio of main to secondary meat, but this is a renegade recipe that is still authentic. If you shape the loaf in a large free-form oval with two separate channels of cheese, it would make an impressive buffet centerpiece, easily serving ten guests. Circle the loaf with slices of avocado, orange, and red onion drizzled with lime vinaigrette. If you try this for your family first, use what doesn't fit your loaf pan to form small meatballs around cubes of cheese and freeze them for canapés—or leave out the cheese altogether.

2 poblano peppers

1 tablespoon canola or other neutral oil

1 small onion, minced

4 garlic cloves, smashed and minced

1 teaspoon ground cumin

2 teaspoons oregano, preferably Mexican

1 tablespoon chipotle peppers in adobo sauce (available in specialty food stores or online)

1 pound ground turkey

1 pound ground pork

1 pound fresh chorizo (a mild supermarket variety is fine)

Kosher salt and freshly ground black pepper

¼ cup minced cilantro, tender stems included

2 eggs, beaten

⅓ cup sour cream

⅔ cup *pepitas* (shelled pumpkin seeds), plus 1 tablespoon for garnish

½ pound mild Cheddar or Monterey Jack in a block roughly 1 inch thick (you'll need more if you are making canapé meatballs—see headnote above)

12 martini-size Manzanilla-stuffed green olives

Char the peppers over an open flame or under the broiler until the skins are black and the peppers have collapsed. Tie them in a plastic bag and when they're cool enough to handle, rub off the skin and pull out the stems, seeds, and veins. Blot them dry and chop very fine or quickly pulse them in a food processor. Set aside.

Heat the oil in a sauté pan and add the onion and garlic. Stir over medium-high heat until the onion is limp but not brown. Add the cumin, oregano, and chipotle pepper and stir to combine. Stir in the roasted poblanos.

Put all the meat in a wide, shallow mixing bowl, slipping the chorizo from its casing—or chop it quickly in a food processor. Lightly combine with a fork and add salt and pepper. Add the onion/chipotle mixture along with the cilantro, eggs, and sour cream. Grind the *pepitas* in a food processor to a coarse meal. Add the *pepitas* to the meat and continue to combine loosely with a fork until all the ingredients are distributed evenly and no clumps of unseasoned meat remain. Knead lightly with your fingers to assure the mixture is well combined.

Preheat the oven to 350°.

Make a small patty with a walnut-size piece of the meat. Sauté it in a little oil and taste for seasoning. Make any necessary adjustments. Fill half of the loaf pan and tap it on the counter to release any air pockets. Cut the cheese into 1-inch-thick logs and place them end to end down the center of the meat. In the same manner, place the olives alongside the cheese. Fill the pan to about ½ inch from the top, pressing down gently, and make a shallow center groove with the side of your hand. Sprinkle the top with the whole pumpkin seeds.

Bake the meat loaf for 1½ hours. Allow it to cool slightly before sliding it out onto a serving platter.

MADEIRA MEAT LOAF with PORCINI and HAZELNUTS

Serves 4

Even a meat loaf deserves a Cinderella transformation once in a while. This one is sumptuous and totally delicious, particularly enriched with the intense mushroom sauce.

$^3/_4$ pound ground chuck
$^1/_4$ pound ground pork
$^1/_4$ pound ground veal
$^1/_3$ cup Madeira
1 cup hot water
2 ounces dried porcini mushrooms, preferably sliced, or a combination of dried mushrooms
7 tablespoons light cream
$^1/_2$ cup stale bread crumbs
$^1/_2$ cup hazelnuts
$1^1/_2$ tablespoons butter, plus more for testing
4 large shallots, minced
3 garlic cloves, minced
$^1/_2$ teaspoon dried thyme

Kosher salt and freshly ground black pepper
$^1/_4$ cup minced flat-leaf parsley
1 egg, beaten
3 thin slices of center-cut bacon

For the Sauce:
2 tablespoons butter
1 shallot, minced
3 tablespoons flour
1 cup soaking liquid from mushrooms
$^1/_3$ cup light cream or half and half
Kosher salt and freshly ground black pepper
Pinch of cayenne pepper

Combine the meats in a wide, shallow bowl and pour the Madeira over them. Toss and allow the meat to marinate.

Pour a cup of hot water over the mushrooms and set aside to soften for about 20 minutes. Pour the cream over the bread crumbs and set them aside as well.

Toast the nuts in a 300° oven for about 10 minutes, or until they release their aroma and appear golden. Rub off as much of their skin as you can in a tea towel and chop them rather finely. Set aside.

Preheat the oven to 350° and take a coffee break.

Heat the butter in a sauté pan and quickly soften the shallots and garlic. Add the thyme and salt and pepper.

Squeeze the mushrooms until almost dry over the soaking water and reserve the water. Chop the mushrooms finely, and sauté a minute or two with the shallot mixture.

Add the bread crumbs, mushroom and shallot mixture, parsley, nuts, and beaten egg to the bowl of marinated meat. Starting with a fork, toss and combine the mixture without compacting it, and then use your fingers to lightly knead it.

Before placing the meat in the pan pinch off a walnut-size patty and sauté it in a little butter. Taste it for seasoning and make any necessary adjustments.

Fill the loaf pan and top the meat with the bacon strips. Bake for 1¼ hours. Allow to cool slightly before attempting to unmold. Serve each slice with a generous drizzle of sauce.

To make the sauce: Melt the butter with the shallot and when the butter starts to foam sprinkle in the flour, whisking rapidly for a few seconds. Strain and heat the mushroom liquid and add it to the roux in small amounts, whisking constantly. When the mixture is satiny smooth, add the cream in the same manner, continuing to whisk until the sauce is lightly thickened. Season and taste. Serve immediately, or store in a covered container with a piece of plastic wrap pressed onto the surface to prevent a skin from forming. The sauce will keep in the fridge for 3 or 4 days. Reheat over low heat or in a double boiler.

LAMB SPIRAL LOAF STUFFED with MINT and FETA

Serves 4 to 6

Filling a meat loaf not only provides interesting flavor options, but the spiral cut is a visual relief from the usual square slice. It's also fun to make and gives rise to creative ideas about how to fill the next one.

1/2 cup minced onion

3 garlic cloves, smashed and minced

2 teaspoons olive oil

1 cup stale bread crumbs soaked in
   1/4 cup milk

1 1/4 pounds ground lamb

1 1/4 teaspoons dried oregano

1/4 cup minced flat-leaf parsley

1/2 teaspoon kosher salt

1/2 teaspoon coarsely ground black
   pepper

1 whole egg plus 1 egg yolk, beaten

1/2 cup chopped mint leaves

1 cup crumbled feta cheese, preferably
   Bulgarian

For the Sauce:

One 14 1/2-ounce can tomatoes,
   preferably Muir Glen Fire-Roasted

1/4 cup dry red wine

1/2 cup chopped mint leaves

1/2 teaspoon dried oregano

Pinch of kosher salt

Freshly ground black pepper

12 Kalamata olives, pitted and split
   (optional)

❧ Preheat the oven to 350°.

Squeeze the onion in a paper towel to remove some of the moisture. Combine it with the garlic and the olive oil in a small dish and microwave for 1 minute on high power, or sauté in a small skillet over medium-high heat about 2 to 3 minutes, until almost soft.

Lightly squeeze the excess milk from the bread crumbs and put the moist crumbs in a wide shallow bowl along with the lamb, oregano, parsley, salt, pepper, beaten egg, and onion/garlic mixture. Lightly distribute all the ingredients with a fork until there are no clumps of unseasoned meat remaining. Work through the mixture thoroughly with your fingers without compacting the meat.

Cut off a 16-inch length of wax paper and center the meat on it. Spread it evenly into an 8 x 12-inch rectangle, patting down gently to remove any air pockets. With a short side facing you, sprinkle the surface with the chopped mint leaves and then with the crumbled cheese, leaving a 1-inch border on the opposite side. Taper the thickness of that border so it will adhere better when it's rolled. Using the paper to lift and turn, roll the meat into a cylinder, gently patting it down as you roll. Press in and flatten the two ragged ends.

Brush a little olive oil on a sheet pan or small roasting pan and carefully lift the meat onto it, using a long spatula for support. Bake the spiral loaf for 1¼ hours.

Lift the meat to a platter or onto a sheet of foil for storage, and scoop out any bits of charred cheese, leaving a couple of tablespoons of the oil and juices in the pan. Put the pan over medium-low heat and add the sauce ingredients. Simmer until the watery liquid has evaporated and the sauce is slightly thickened. Use immediately or cool to store. The sauce will keep several days in the fridge.

COOK'S NOTES: *For a spectacular Greek-inspired company presentation, roll the baked and cooled loaf in eight buttered leaves of phyllo dough, following the instructions on the box, and return it to a preheated 375° oven to brown and crisp for about 20 minutes. You can also wrap packages of individual slices so your guests get more of the crispy phyllo.*

SOUR CREAM and HORSERADISH MEAT LOAF with GLAZED ROASTED BEETS

Serves 6

*S*ince the advent of the roasted beet, I've been on a mission to convert beet haters. I'm particularly fond of them glazed with balsamic vinegar, and in this recipe their garnet gloss looks stunning trapped between thin strips of green. For once, they can't bloodstain their neighbors on the dinner plate.

I can never resist buying the gnarly horseradish root, but I can never seem to get rid of it either. This is a good excuse to buy one. Its bite is more lingeringly subtle than the vinegary bottled horseradish, which would add unnecessary acidity to this meat loaf. If you must use it bottled, drain and rinse it under cool water in a small strainer and pat it dry before adding it.

2 to 3 big leaves of red Swiss chard
4 small to medium beets,
    about 1 bunch
Balsamic vinegar
1/4 cup minced onion
3 garlic cloves, smashed and minced
Olive oil for drizzling
1 pound ground chuck
1/2 pound ground pork
1 teaspoon kosher salt

1/2 teaspoon coarsely ground black
    pepper
1/4 cup minced flat-leaf parsley
1 1/4 teaspoons dried dill weed
1 egg
1/4 cup grated fresh horseradish or
    2 tablespoons bottled
1/2 cup sour cream
5 slices of center-cut bacon

◞ Blanch the chard in rapidly boiling water, drain, and cut out the thick stems.

Preheat the oven to 350° and cut off the leaves and stems of the beets to within an inch of the top, leaving their tails intact. (You can also use a toaster oven.) Roast them for an hour and a half. The skins will shrivel and the caramelized beets will have shrunk inside. When they're cool enough to handle, slip off the skins and slice them about ⅜ inch thick. Lay the slices in a single layer in a skillet and pour in a couple of tablespoons of balsamic vinegar. Turn the heat to medium and when the vinegar starts sizzling, flip the slices over. Remove from the heat when the beets are glazed and the vinegar has evaporated.

Blot the excess moisture from the minced onion and mix it with the garlic in a small microwave-proof dish. Drizzle on a few drops of oil and cook on high for 30 seconds. Scrape the softened onion into a wide shallow bowl and add the meat, salt, pepper, parsley, and one teaspoon of the dill weed. Whisk together the egg, horseradish, and sour cream and add to the meat. Combine with a fork, keeping the mixture loose, until there are no unseasoned patches of meat. Use your fingers to knead the mixture gently but thoroughly.

Form a walnut-size piece of meat into a patty. Sauté it quickly in a little oil and taste for seasoning and cohesion. Make any necessary adjustments.

Line a 9 x 5-inch loaf pan with two slices of bacon and fill the pan with half the meat. Slit half the chard leaves to cover the surface and fit the beet slices on top, leaving no cracks. Sprinkle them with the remaining ¼ teaspoon of dill and a little salt and pepper. Encase the beets with the remaining chard leaves and fill the pan with the other half of the meat, gently pressing down all around to form a seal. Top with the remaining bacon and bake for 1¼ hours. Pour off the juices and allow to cool slightly before serving, or cool completely for storage.

COOK'S NOTES: *For added glamour, bake the meat loaf for an hour and allow it to cool to room temperature or store it overnight. Bring it back to room temperature and enclose it in the Sour Cream Turnover Pastry (page 177), following the procedure for Finnish Meat Loaf en Croûte (page 68). Bake for 30 to 40 minutes until golden. Serve hot or cold.*

FINNISH MEAT LOAF en CROÛTE

Serves 4 to 6

As you might imagine, this satisfying dish was very popular with Finnish embassy personnel whenever we featured it on the menu at my Washington restaurant, The Big Cheese. One of my favorite comic kitchen memories was that of my featherweight first cook perched precariously on a bar stool with a steel bowl wider than her shoulders gripped between her knees while she mixed up 15 pounds of filling at a clip. With every toss the stool tipped forward and nearly pitched her to the floor.

In Finland, where this popular meat loaf is a common fast-food item in train and bus stations, it's called *lihamurekepiiras*, a tongue twister I mischievously printed on the menu without translation. Instead of serving a slice with the traditional lingonberry preserves and sour cream, you could easily bake it as individual turnovers. It's as delicious at room temperature as it is hot.

3 tablespoons butter
1/3 cup minced onion
1/2 cup minced cremini mushrooms
Kosher salt and freshly ground black
    pepper
1/2 teaspoon dried thyme
3/4 pound ground chuck
1/4 pound ground pork
1/4 pound ground veal

1/4 pound ground smoked ham
1/4 cup minced flat-leaf parsley
1/2 cup grated Gruyère cheese
1 egg, lightly beaten with 1/4 cup milk
    or light cream
1 recipe Sour Cream Turnover Pastry
    (page 177)
1 egg, for glaze

〰 Melt the butter in a large sauté pan. Squeeze the onion of its excess liquid in a paper towel and add it to the pan with the mushrooms, salt, pepper, and thyme. Toss and stir until all the liquid is evaporated.

Combine all the meat in a wide shallow bowl with a fork, without compacting it. Add the meat to the sauté pan over medium-high heat and combine it with the mushroom mixture. Chop through the mixture with a wooden spoon just until all redness turns pale gray.

Remove the mixture to a wide shallow bowl with a slotted spoon, leaving the juice behind. Add the parsley and the grated cheese and combine. Allow the mixture to cool before adding the beaten egg. Work it lightly through the meat with your fingers. On a sheet of heavy-duty foil, form the meat into a half-round cylinder roughly 3 inches across the bottom. Or, you can make a long, narrow rectangle. Keep the shape narrow so each slice has more dough to hold it in shape. Refrigerate the loaf for at least an hour or as long as overnight. You can also freeze it wrapped tightly in foil, to be wrapped in dough later.

Whenever you're ready to assemble the loaf, preheat the oven to 375°.

Cut off one-third of the chilled dough and roll it on a floured surface into a rectangle that will allow a 1-inch border around the meat. Put it in the middle of a cookie sheet and save the scraps.

Roll the remaining dough into a rectangle large enough to drape over the top of the meat and meet the borders. Once you have a good fit, whisk the egg with a dash of water and moisten the bottom border. Crimp and seal all four sides with the tines of a fork. Roll out any scraps and cut into strips to crisscross over the top, or cut into other decorative shapes. Glue them down with a touch of the egg wash and use the rest to brush over the top of the loaf. Bake for 30 minutes or until the crust is golden brown.

Serve each slice with lingonberry preserves and sour cream or just sour cream mixed with horseradish.

PORK MEATBALLS with ORANGE PLUMS and ALMONDS

Serves 4

Considering the well-established nutritional qualities of dried plums—aka prunes—as well as those of almonds, sage, and garlic, these meatballs could be called medicine balls.

This well-seasoned pork, studded with fruit and nuts, is delicious served over buttered egg noodles.

8 dried orange plums, soaked in orange juice

1 cup crustless bread crumbs, soaked in milk

2 tablespoons canola or other neutral oil

1/3 cup minced shallots

3 garlic cloves, smashed and minced

1 teaspoon kosher salt

1 teaspoon coarse black pepper

8 leaves of fresh sage, minced

1/3 cup minced flat-leaf parsley

1 1/2 pounds ground pork

1/3 cup slivered almonds, toasted and finely chopped

1 egg

1 tablespoon Dijon mustard

Set the plums and bread crumbs aside to soften. Heat the oil and briefly sauté the shallots and garlic. Add the salt, pepper, sage, and parsley. Stir to combine. Place the pork in a wide shallow bowl and add the seasonings along with the toasted almonds, the plums (drained and minced) and the bread crumbs (lightly squeezed of excess milk). Combine all the ingredients thoroughly with a fork without compacting the meat. Whisk the egg with the mustard and a little of the soaking milk from the bread and add it to the bowl.

Use your fingers to lightly knead the meat, assuring a good mix. Sauté a small patty of the meat; taste it and make any needed adjustments to the seasoning or consistency.

Form the mixture into Ping-Pong–size balls and sauté them in a 2-to-1 combination of oil and butter until they're golden brown and thoroughly cooked. Serve immediately; or cool, refrigerate, or freeze.

SPICY CHICKEN SAUSAGE and HAM MEATBALLS

*I*t *is the unusual variety of meat and seasonings* that makes these meatballs memorable. Serve them with the Herbed Sweet Potato and Celeriac Gratin (page 107) or the Red Cabbage with Shallots and Dried Cherries (page 102.)

½ cup minced onion
1 tablespoon canola oil
1 teaspoon Curry Powder (page 123)
1 teaspoon ground ginger
1 teaspoon dry mustard
¼ teaspoon nutmeg
Kosher salt and freshly ground black
   pepper

½ pound fresh chicken sausage
½ pound ground baked ham
¼ pound ground pork
1 cup whole grain or sourdough fresh
   bread crumbs
1 tablespoon lime juice
1 egg, beaten
½ cup sour cream

 Wring the excess water from the onion in a paper towel. Heat the oil and sauté the onion for 1 minute before adding the Curry Powder, ginger, mustard, nutmeg, salt, and pepper. Sauté another minute or so and set aside.

Rather than scraping the sausage from its casing, you can break it up in the food processor after processing the ham. Place the ham, sausage, and pork in a wide shallow bowl and combine lightly with a fork without compacting the meat. Add the seasoning mixture along with the bread crumbs and lime juice and continue combining the ingredients. Whisk the beaten egg into the sour cream and add it to the bowl. Briefly mix it with a fork and then use your fingers to lightly work the mixture together.

Roll a piece of the mixture into a walnut-size ball and sauté in a couple of drops of oil. Taste it for seasoning and consistency and make any necessary adjustments.

Form the rest of the meat into any size meatballs and sauté them until golden. You can freeze any you don't plan to use within 3 to 4 days.

SAIGON MEATBALLS

Serves 4

These subtly spiced, tender meatballs would be quite authentic skewered, grilled, and served with Asian Peanut Sauce (page 129), Sweet Pineapple and Cucumber Salad with Daikon (page 96), and jasmine rice. They're also delectable steamed on napa cabbage or poached in homemade Chicken Broth (page 4) and served on a nest of rice noodles. They would make ideal cocktail canapés so you might consider doubling this recipe and freezing the leftovers for your next party.

½ teaspoon Thai or Vietnamese sriracha sauce (available in Asian or specialty food stores)

1 teaspoon canola oil

2 teaspoons pureed Roasted Garlic (page 155) or 1 teaspoon minced raw

2 teaspoons grated gingerroot

5 green onions, trimmed, leaving an inch of the green

Freshly ground black pepper

2 tablespoons Asian fish sauce (*nam pla or nuoc mam*)

1½ teaspoons sugar

1 egg

1 tablespoon cornstarch

1 pound ground pork

 Place all the ingredients except the cornstarch and pork into the bowl of a food processor or blender. Pulse to combine until smooth.

Sprinkle the cornstarch over the pork from a small sieve, folding it in until it disappears. Add the meat to the food processor and pulse the mixture to a smooth paste. Test a small sautéed patty and make any seasoning adjustments before refrigerating the mixture for at least an hour or freezing for later use.

Moisten your hands and form the meat into bite-size balls for grilling, sautéing, or steaming. (The meatballs can be successfully steamed in the microwave.)

THE NEW CHICKEN CROQUETTE

Serves 4

*A*s mentioned in the chapter introduction, there's a simple way to lighten the traditional croquette, and that is by using a vegetable puree in lieu of the thick béchamel to bind the ingredients. The vegetable puree does alter its character, but unlike some other healthy makeovers, this one is as good as, if not better than, the original. If you have bad croquette karma, this should redefine them for you, and if you've never had one, you might want to start with these.

Since all the ingredients are precooked, the mixture keeps well in the refrigerator for several days but cannot be successfully frozen.

1 small head of cauliflower	2 teaspoons Worcestershire sauce
1 cup milk	3 tablespoons minced chives
1 tablespoon soft butter	Pinch of cayenne pepper
Kosher salt and freshly ground black pepper	Flour for rolling the croquettes
1/4 cup finely diced carrot	1 egg, beaten
2 cups minced cooked chicken	Fine dry bread crumbs, preferably Japanese *panko*
2 tablespoons minced flat-leaf parsley	

❧ Trim the cauliflower of its thick stems and separate the florets. Place them in a microwave-proof gratin dish and pour in the milk. Cover the dish with plastic wrap and steam at 70 percent power for 8 minutes or until the tip of a knife pierces the florets easily. Allow the cauliflower to cool slightly, remove it to a food processor with a slotted spoon, and puree it with the butter, salt, and pepper. Measure out 1 cup of the mixture for the croquettes and place it in a wide shallow bowl.

Place the remaining puree back in the processor with some of the milk and blend again until silky smooth, fluffy, and white. Store this to reheat—it's perfectly delicious under a grilled fish fillet.

Steam the carrot in the microwave until barely tender and add it to the cauliflower. Add the chicken, parsley, Worcestershire, chives, and cayenne and thoroughly combine. Taste for seasoning and adjust if necessary. Chill the mixture until it's firm enough to form into cylinders, pyramids, or spheres.

Roll the croquettes in flour, then in the beaten egg, and coat them completely with the crumbs. (Because this croquette is moist and delicate, you'll need a sturdy crust to prevent interior steam from exploding it in the hot oil.) Chill the breaded croquettes, uncovered, preferably overnight.

If you choose to bake them, preheat the oven to 425°. Drizzle some oil into a baking pan and roll the croquettes in it to lightly coat the crumbs, or use a spray oil. Bake for 15 minutes and then roll them over to brown uniformly. Bake another 20 minutes until golden and crisp.

To shallow-fry, bring the croquettes to room temperature and heat 1½ inches of the oil in a wok or Dutch oven until a candy thermometer reaches 375°. Drop in the croquettes without allowing them to touch.

Line a cookie pan with paper towels and place a cooling rack over it. The croquettes should turn deep brown in about 8 minutes. Lift them onto the rack. (The inside of a croquette stays steaming hot for a long time, so if you're working in relays, you needn't worry about keeping them warm.) If you're frying a large number, however, you can keep the croquettes warm in a 250° oven.

COOK'S NOTES: *To complement the fresh taste of these croquettes, serve them over a small ladleful of Lemon-Chive Sauce (page 143). Don't cover them with sauce or the crust will be soggy.*

There are innumerable variations possible with this basic recipe. The puree can be made from broccoli, beans, chickpeas, or mashed potato. You can add almost any cooked and diced meat, seafood, or cheese, along with your favorite herbs. You can try different sauces such as a roasted red pepper puree with a dash of cream or Tomato Concassé (page 142).

PORTUGUESE SHRIMP CROQUETTES

Serves 4

T*his is my idea of the ultimate croquette.* With so many of my favorite ingredients blended together and oozing from a thick crunchy crust, these are as good as croquettes get.

2 tablespoons extra-virgin olive oil
1/3 cup minced onion
2 garlic cloves, smashed and minced
1/4 teaspoon dried oregano
1/3 cup minced red bell pepper
1/2 cup peeled, seeded, and pulped,
    minced tomato
1/3 cup minced flat-leaf parsley
1/4 cup chopped almonds, toasted
2 cups diced cooked shrimp
Kosher salt and freshly ground
    black pepper

2 slices white toast, crumbled and
    soaked in 1/2 cup milk
3 tablespoons butter
3 tablespoons flour
1 tablespoon Madeira
1 1/4 cups milk
Flour, plus 2 beaten eggs for coating
Fine dry bread crumbs, preferably
    Japanese *panko*
Canola oil for frying

❧ Heat the oil and sauté the onion and garlic until soft. Add the oregano, red pepper, tomato, parsley, almonds, shrimp, salt, pepper, and the toast, after squeezing out the excess milk.

Combine thoroughly and turn the mixture out into a bowl. Wipe out the pan and heat the butter in it. Add the flour, whisking constantly, over medium heat until a smooth roux forms. Continue to cook for another 2 minutes, pulling the pot off the heat as necessary to keep from scorching. Add the Madeira, allowing it to sizzle before whisking it in. Slowly add the milk and continue to whisk. Once the sauce is smooth, simmer it gently for about 10 minutes or until it becomes thick.

Blot any visible moisture from the shrimp mixture and fold the cream sauce into it. Spread evenly in a flat dish and chill until firm.

Shape the croquettes into cylinders, pyramids, or spheres. Coat them lightly with flour before dipping them in the beaten eggs. Finally, turn them over repeatedly in the bread crumbs. A complete seal will keep the oil from seeping inside.

To bake the croquettes, preheat the oven to 425°. Brush or spray a film of oil on a baking pan and roll the croquettes onto it, lightly coating the crumbs. Bake the croquettes for about 15 minutes and then roll them over to brown uniformly. Bake another 20 minutes until they're golden and crisp.

To shallow-fry, bring the croquettes to room temperature and heat 1½ inches of oil in a wok or Dutch oven until a candy thermometer reaches 375°. Drop the croquettes in the oil without allowing them to touch each other.

Line a baking pan with paper towels and place a cooling rack over it. The croquettes should reach a deep brown in about 8 minutes. Lift them onto the rack with a slotted spoon. (The inside of a croquette stays steaming hot for a long time, so if you're working in relays, you needn't worry about keeping them warm.) If you're frying a large number, however, you can keep the croquettes warm in a 250° oven.

COOK'S NOTES: *I like to serve these croquettes with a dollop of light mayonnaise seasoned with fresh lemon juice, Roasted Garlic (page 155), and minced cilantro.*

In place of the shrimp, you can substitute cooked salmon, cod, crab, or chopped clams. A little dab of hollandaise sauce served under each croquette would be splendid.

LAMB CROQUETTES with CURRIED POTATOES and PEAS

Makes 12 large croquettes or
8 large and 8 small

I recently discovered a small container of vegetable samosa filling in my refrigerator, left over from a party, along with some ground lamb in urgent need of cooking. This simplified recipe makes use of both.

1 tablespoon butter	Cayenne pepper to taste (optional)
1 tablespoon canola oil	1/4 cup frozen baby peas, thawed
1 garlic clove, smashed and minced	1/4 cup light cream or half and half
2 tablespoons minced onion	3/4 pound ground lamb
1 cup boiled potato cut in 1/4 -inch dice	1 egg, beaten
2 teaspoons grated gingerroot	Flour, for dusting the croquettes
1 teaspoon garam masala	2 eggs, lightly beaten, for dipping the
2 teaspoons Curry Powder (page 123)	croquettes
Kosher salt and freshly ground black	Fine dry bread crumbs, preferably
pepper	Japanese *panko*

Heat the butter and oil and sauté the garlic and onion until wilted. Add the potato, ginger, garam masala, Curry Powder, salt, and pepper. Stir to combine over medium-low heat to release the aromatic spices. Taste for seasoning. This should be spicy enough to season the rest of the ingredients. If not, add the cayenne. Add the peas and the cream. Stir to combine and remove from the heat to cool.

Place the meat in a wide shallow bowl with the beaten egg and potato mixture. Salt again and combine with a fork. Use your fingers to completely distribute the ingredients.

Form the mixture into cylinders, pyramids, or spheres and lightly dust with flour. Dip the croquettes first into the beaten eggs and then coat them thoroughly in the crumbs. Bake in a preheated 400° oven for 35 minutes, or shallow-fry for 8 minutes as instructed in the previous croquette recipes.

HAM and EGG CROQUETTES

Serves 4

I couldn't resist offering one more béchamel-based croquette, because they make such a sensu-ous and satisfying presentation for either brunch or supper. These would pair perfectly with grilled spring asparagus or minted fresh baby peas.

Béchamel Base:
2 tablespoons butter
4 tablespoons flour
Kosher salt and white pepper
1 cup milk, 2 percent or evaporated
    skim
2 tablespoons grated Parmigiano-
    Reggiano

4 hard-boiled eggs, minced
1½ ounces smoked ham, minced
¼ cup diced Fontina cheese
Flour, plus 2 beaten eggs for coating
Fine dry bread crumbs, or Japanese
    panko

Melt the butter and whisk in the flour to make a roux. Add salt and pepper. Cook over medium heat for a couple of minutes without allowing it to brown. Add the milk slowly, whisk-ing constantly, until the sauce is smooth and starts to thicken. Simmer for 10 minutes until the béchamel is quite thick. Stir in the Parmigiano-Reggiano. Remove from the heat, place a piece of plastic wrap on the surface to prevent a skin from forming, and allow the sauce to cool com-pletely.

Combine the hard-boiled eggs, ham, and Fontina cheese and fold in ½ cup of the béchamel. At this point the mixture can be stored in the refrigerator for several days. You can freeze the leftover béchamel for another use.

When you're ready to serve, form eight spherical croquettes and roll them in the flour. Brush off the excess and dip them into the beaten eggs, coating them all around. Finally, turn them over on a plate of dry bread crumbs, pressing the crumbs lightly into the croquette to assure a thick shell.

Fry the croquettes, four at a time, in 1½ inches of oil heated to 375° on a candy thermome-ter, for 3 minutes on each side. Keep the first batch warm in a 250° oven on a rack over paper towels.

COOK'S NOTES: *For a more elegant version, substitute slivered prosciutto for the smoked ham.*

Do not overcook the hard-boiled eggs. The yolks should be bright yellow and moist, not pale and chalky with that hated green rim. To achieve the best results, ignore the name "hard-boiled" and never cook the eggs above a gentle simmer. Twelve minutes after the eggs are dropped in and the water returns to a simmer, should do it. A quick plunge into cold water will stop further cooking and make the eggs easier to peel. The fresher the egg, the more stubborn the shell. Holding the egg under cold water to peel usually forces the membrane to release along with the shell, leaving the white of the egg unmarred.

COUNTRY-STYLE SAUSAGE
with ROSEMARY

Makes one 2¼ x 6-inch sausage

Making your own sausage is incredibly simple and satisfying. You don't need any special equipment, and there's no need to encase the sausage in those slippery pig intestines. Best of all, you control the quality of ingredients, the amount of fat, and a world of seasoning choices. This low-fat spicy bulk sausage can be made too quickly to qualify for serious weekend cooking, but if it inspires you to experiment one day with several different flavors and shapes, you will have added another worthwhile do-ahead project to your repertoire. Bulk sausage has myriad uses, not only with potato pancakes and fruited red cabbage but in some casseroles and stuffings for poultry or vegetables. A soft cheese omelet with a patty of spicy country sausage is a fine weekday supper.

1 pound ground pork, preferably ground once

1 teaspoon kosher salt

½ teaspoon coarsely ground black pepper

2 teaspoons minced rosemary leaves

1 teaspoon dried thyme

½ teaspoon Spanish smoked paprika (*pimentón*)

¼ teaspoon cayenne pepper, or to taste

❧ Place all of the ingredients in a wide shallow bowl and combine thoroughly with your fingers. Pull off a walnut-size ball of meat, sauté it in a little oil, and taste for seasoning. Make adjustments to suit your palate.

At this point, you can form patties to use within a day or two, or you can wrap them tightly and freeze for use as is, or to complete another dish.

Alternatively, you can knead the mixture into a dense cylinder and roll it first into a length of microwave-safe plastic wrap and then into aluminum foil, twisting the ends. Allow the sausage to macerate in the refrigerator overnight.

Remove the foil wrapper and secure the plastic wrap, or rewrap tightly. The sausage should feel solid and be smoothly shaped. Make a couple of pinpricks through the plastic wrap on the top side of the cylinder and place it in a covered microwave steamer or dish with ¼ inch of water. Microwave on 70 percent power for 12 minutes. Oven wattage varies, so it's wise to cut through the middle to check for doneness. No pink should remain, and the internal temperature must reach 155°. If it needs more time, rewrap and return it to the oven. Make notes for the next time. You can also steam or poach the sausage conventionally, wrapped in cheesecloth or plastic wrap and again in foil. It will take about 30 minutes. Again, check the internal temperature to be safe.

Now you have cooked sausage that will keep for a week wrapped and refrigerated, or several weeks frozen. Cut it in thick slices and brown it in a little oil to serve hot, or slice thinly and serve cold on a cheese board or with garlicky toast for canapés. Don't forget the gherkins and pickled onions.

COOK'S NOTES: *If you miss the traditional richness of pork sausage or you grind lean meat, you can add a half cup of minced pork fat to the mixture, but I find regular ground pork contains enough fat to avoid dryness. The texture is denser but enjoying it thinly sliced cold is a great trade-off.*

If you buy the pork in a piece to grind yourself, select butt, shoulder, or boned country ribs. If you grind the meat in the food processor, cut it in cubes and pulse in small quantities. Don't overprocess.

You can make link shapes following the same procedure but eliminating the foil wrap. Twist the plastic between links and tie with string. Place them around the outside edge of a Pyrex pie plate with a little water in the bottom, or cook in a steamer basket on top of the stove. Remove the wrappers before browning the links slowly in a well-oiled sauté pan, or toss them on the outdoor grill, away from direct heat, to pick up a delicious smoky taste.

MEXICAN GREEN CHORIZO

This is a bulk sausage redolent with the fresh green herbs and bold seasonings we associate with Mexican food. Crumble it on tacos, serve it in patties with a simple rice pilaf, or mix it with leftover cooked rice or beans to stuff tomatoes. Although I've included optional pork fat, fresh pork back fat is hard to find. Salt pork is not a substitute, but lean chorizo packs so much flavor you'll hardly miss the fat.

- ⅓ cup rice wine or white wine vinegar
- 6 garlic cloves, smashed and chopped
- 2 teaspoons dried oregano
- ¼ teaspoon cayenne pepper
- 2 teaspoons ground cumin
- 2 teaspoons kosher salt
- 2 poblano peppers, roasted, peeled, and seeded

- 3 serrano peppers, stemmed and seeded
- 1 cup loosely packed chopped flat-leaf parsley
- 1 cup chopped cilantro (thick stems removed)
- 2 pounds ground pork
- ½ pound ground pork back fat (optional) (see headnote above)

❧ Place all the ingredients except the meat and pork fat into a food processor and puree. Place the meat and pork fat, if you are using it, into a wide shallow mixing bowl, add the seasoning puree, and combine first with a fork and then with your fingers to incorporate the ingredients. Refrigerate overnight before using. The uncooked chorizo will keep for 3 days in the refrigerator or can be frozen for several weeks.

COOK'S NOTES: *See Country-Style Sausage with Rosemary, page 80, for instructions on how to form and precook the sausage for longer storage.*

MINCED CLAM and PROSCIUTTO BREAD STUFFING

Makes 5 cups

This is a terrific, flavorful filling, particularly for big, thick portobello mushrooms for a main dish or smaller stuffing mushrooms for a first course or canapés. It would also make an unusual, zesty filling for Cornish hens or a whole fish.

5 tablespoons unsalted butter

1/2 cup minced shallots

3 garlic cloves, smashed and minced

2 tender celery stalks, minced

1/4 cup minced mixed fresh herbs, such as thyme, sage, and oregano

1/4 cup minced flat-leaf parsley

2 slices prosciutto, thinly slivered and chopped

Two 6 1/2 -ounce cans minced clams, drained, with juice reserved

1/2 teaspoon lemon juice

Pinch of cayenne pepper

5 cups torn stale bread crumbs with the crusts

Kosher salt and freshly ground black pepper

1 egg, beaten with 1 tablespoon cream or milk

Grated Parmigiano-Reggiano

 Heat the butter and sauté the shallots and garlic until soft. Add the celery and sauté until barely tender. Add the herbs, prosciutto, clams, lemon juice, cayenne, bread crumbs. Toss well to combine while drizzling in the reserved clam juice to moisten the mixture. If the mixture needs more liquid add a little cream or milk. Add the pepper but taste before adding the salt, since the clams and prosciutto are both salty.

If you don't use this stuffing right away you can store it in a tightly covered container for 4 days. When you're ready to serve it, stir in the beaten egg.

Sprinkle the grated cheese on top if you're stuffing mushrooms—or fold some in if you're stuffing hens or onions.

HERBED ORZO and SAUSAGE STUFFING

Makes about 4 cups

W*hen I think of stuffed vegetables*, I'm reminded of the most visually appetizing antipasto buffet I've ever seen. It was on the craggy island of Sardinia in the partially open-air dining pavilion of a designer's dream of a hotel. Maybe it was the sun-streaked dazzle of the whitewashed walls or the background slice of teal blue Mediterranean that heightened my sensitivities, but I really think it was the stuffed vegetables. Long tables with bleached white cloths were set end to end with equally stark white platters of tomatoes, onions, peppers, zucchini, baby eggplant, celery, artichokes, mushrooms, fennel, and more. Each vegetable was stuffed differently. Their brilliant colors glistened with olive oil and their herbaceous perfume drew me closer to the table. I paused for a second—then grabbed a big fork.

3 tablespoons extra-virgin olive oil
2 tablespoons minced onion
3 garlic cloves, smashed and minced
Pinch of dried red pepper flakes, or to taste
4 ounces Italian sweet sausage, chopped
2 plum tomatoes, peeled, seeded, and chopped

1 tablespoon chopped oregano leaves
3 tablespoons minced flat-leaf parsley
Kosher salt and freshly ground black pepper
3 cups cooked and cooled orzo or Arborio rice
1 egg, beaten

Heat the oil in a skillet and sauté the onion and garlic until softened. Add the pepper flakes and the sausage. Push down on the meat with the edge of a wooden spoon to break up any large clumps. Cook until no traces of raw meat remain. Add the tomatoes, herbs, and seasoning. Combine and simmer until the mixture is more cohesive, pouring off any excess oil or fat but leaving behind enough to moisten the orzo.

Fold in the orzo and combine well. If you don't plan to use the stuffing right away, you can refrigerate it in a covered container for several days or freeze it.

When you're ready to use the stuffing, mix in the beaten egg and fill the chosen casings.

COOK'S NOTES: *This stuffing is very versatile and can be used to fill tomatoes, onions, peppers, winter or summer squash, or a roasting chicken.*

If you're using the stuffing for vegetables, sprinkle the tops with fresh bread crumbs, drizzle with olive oil, and dust with grated Parmigiano-Reggiano or aged Asiago cheese.

EGGPLANT and BULGUR STUFFING

Makes about 4 cups

Eggplant deserves more attention than it gets. Stuffed with its own seasoned flesh it's delicious, but stuffing it into tomatoes, onions, or bell peppers is equally so. I crave eggplant in any form in spite of its drab appearance and occasional bitterness. Encasing the pulp in a more glamorous vegetable solves the former problem, and using the petite, less seedy Italian eggplant—or the virtually seedless Asian variety—solves the latter.

Eggplant isn't exactly a no-fuss, quick-cook vegetable. Thankfully, it often gains in flavor from refrigerator storage so lends itself well to do-ahead preparation.

2 medium eggplant or 4 small Italian or Asian	1 teaspoon dried mint
Kosher salt	½ teaspoon ground cumin
¼ cup olive oil	½ cup V8 juice
¼ cup minced onion	1½ cups cooked bulgur
1 teaspoon turmeric	1 cup yogurt
	1 egg, beaten

 Peel the eggplant unless you're using the Asian variety that has a more tender edible skin. Cut the flesh into small cubes and place it in a colander. Sprinkle with salt and toss. Leave the eggplant to drain for about an hour. (The salting is not so much to reduce bitterness, which I'm not totally convinced works, but to prevent the eggplant from absorbing too much oil.)

Heat the oil and sauté the eggplant over medium-high heat, shaking and tossing to brown and soften the flesh. Add more oil if you need to, to prevent sticking. Eggplant has a habit of exuding absorbed oil after it's removed from the heat.

When the tip of a knife pierces the cubes easily, remove the eggplant to a mixing bowl with a sheet of paper towel in the bottom. Sauté the onion briefly and add the turmeric, mint, cumin, and V8. Simmer for a minute or two to release the aroma of the spices and evaporate the liquid by about half. Pull out the oily paper towel and pour in the onion mixture, bulgur, and yogurt. Combine all the ingredients well.

If you aren't using the stuffing right away, you can safely store it in a covered container for several days. When you're ready to fill your chosen vegetables, add the beaten egg and toss to coat.

MUSHROOM and ONION STUFFING

Makes about 4 cups

This is a very simple and very tasty filling for onions, summer squash, tomatoes, poultry, and fish. The base mushroom and onion mixture keeps for days in the refrigerator and can be frozen as well. You can use it to season a bread stuffing, as I've done here, and bake it alone as a side dish. Or, mix the stuffing into a baked potato, or simply top grilled meat or fish. Sometimes we forget the classics in our search for something new.

6 thin slices of center-cut smoked
  bacon, slivered
3 tablespoons butter
1 large Vidalia or Texas sweet onion,
  finely chopped
1/4 cup minced parsley
1 tablespoon fresh thyme leaves
Pinch of cayenne pepper

2 cups finely chopped cremini mushrooms
Kosher salt and freshly ground black
  pepper
1/4 teaspoon freshly grated nutmeg
2 cups crumbled stale bread crumbs
1 egg, beaten with 2 tablespoons cream
  or milk

Sauté the bacon until cooked but not crisp; set aside. Pour off all but 2 tablespoons of the fat and add 1 tablespoon of the butter and the onion. Sauté until the onion is soft but not brown. Add the parsley, thyme, and cayenne. Stir to combine and set aside in a mixing bowl.

Melt the remaining butter and sauté the mushrooms over medium-high heat, tossing and stirring until the mushrooms pick up a golden tinge. Add the salt, pepper, and grated nutmeg. Add the bacon and mushrooms to the onions and mix well. At this point you can store the mixture in the refrigerator or freeze it.

When, and if, you choose to use it as a bread stuffing, add the crumbs and the egg.

MEXICAN RICE and CHEESE STUFFING

Makes about 4 cups

This stuffing was born to fill poblano peppers, but it would do well baked in onion shells or in the cavity of a roasting chicken.

2 cups leftover cooked rice
Kosher salt and freshly ground black
   pepper
2 plum tomatoes, peeled, seeded, and
   finely chopped

½ cup crumbled dry chorizo
¾ cup grated Monterey Jack cheese
¼ cup minced flat-leaf parsley
¼ cup minced cilantro
1 egg, beaten

Combine all the ingredients except the egg with a fork. Add the egg just before using the filling. Otherwise, you can refrigerate it for several days in a covered container. Do not freeze.

COOK'S NOTES: *Chorizo varies in spiciness. If yours is not hot enough, add a minced jalapeño or serrano pepper to the mix. Bottled pickled jalapeños are even hotter.*

TROPICAL TURKEY STUFFING

For a 12- to 15-pound bird

One recent Thanksgiving I was so underwhelmed by the thought of roasting the same old traditional bird that I devised this stuffing to amuse myself and, hopefully, please my guests. It was a thumbs-up hit and even the turkey looked proud. There must be other culinary iconoclasts willing to risk a raised eyebrow or two in return for applause. The quality of ingredients is key and well worth a fresh, naturally fed bird. You can halve the recipe and try it out in a roasting chicken first or bake it separately as an unusual side dish.

1 large white sweet onion, minced

8 garlic cloves, smashed and minced

1 habañero pepper, seeded and minced

1½ cups mixed dried, unglazed tropical fruit, such as mango, papaya, pineapple

½ cup currants soaked in 3 tablespoons dark rum

½ cup chopped Brazil nuts

1 cup salted macadamia nuts, chopped and lightly toasted

1 small bunch of flat-leaf parsley, chopped

2 bunches of chives, snipped

1 bunch of cilantro, chopped

10 cups rough chunks from a variety of dry bakery bread, such as sourdough, whole wheat, 7-grain, and pumpernickel

Kosher salt and freshly ground black pepper

1 cup (2 sticks) melted butter

Turkey or Chicken Broth (page 4), homemade or canned

☙ Combine all the ingredients and adjust the degree of moisture with the broth. The crunchy texture and lively seasonings make this stuffing better suited to a somewhat dry finish, as it takes pan gravy well.

COOK'S NOTES: *If you use this stuffing in a turkey or chicken, glaze the bird with a small jar of currant jelly melted with 2 tablespoons dark rum and a few drops of Tabasco.*

To add further to the eccentricities of this recipe, make your pan gravy by whisking ¼ cup flour into the pan drippings, scraping up all the brown bits. Salt and pepper the roux. After it has cooked for a couple of minutes, add a cup of strong coffee and as much broth as it takes to reach your preferred consistency. Add ¼ cup of milk at the end to smooth out the flavor and perfect the color.

SOME TIPS FOR STUFFING VEGETABLES

Peppers: Select thick-skinned peppers for stuffing, such as bell, poblano, or Italian long peppers. Thin skins can too easily burst. Although preroasting and peeling peppers will most likely compromise their shape, they taste much better roasted, and the finished peppers will cut more easily. Blanch them in boiling water for 5 minutes and, after stuffing, broil them on their sides to char the skins. Or, char them first over an open flame or under the broiler as quickly as possible to prevent collapse; rub off the papery black skin, stuff, and bake.

Onions: The center of the onion can most easily be reamed out with a melon baller. Always blanch the shells before stuffing and baking.

Mushrooms: Raw mushrooms contain a lot of moisture and will leak into the stuffing, making it soggy. Broil the mushrooms briefly to release some of the water, and blot them well before stuffing.

Eggplant: If you try to bake a whole eggplant and then scoop out the flesh for stuffing, often the shell will be so collapsed you'll have difficulty stuffing it. You can solve that problem by scooping the raw flesh out, leaving a thin layer around the shell, and then proceeding to make the stuffing. Drizzled with oil, the shell will soften when it's filled and baked.

General Tip: To keep small round vegetables upright while filling and in the oven, try standing them up in a Texas-size muffin tin or a Bundt pan.

SIDE DISHES

4

More often than not when we think about what to have for dinner we think only of meat, fish, or poultry—the accompaniments remain afterthoughts. We used to feel obligated to follow the proper meat-and-two-vegetables ratio. When we no longer had time to wait around for the family roast, we switched to the broiled steak and foil-wrapped potato—with or without a tossed green salad. Now increased nutritional awareness, and even less time to cook, has led us to the salmon, chicken breast, and broccoli syndrome. Both limited time and health pressures make it harder and harder to think out of the minimalist box.

Surely, it's a good thing that we've drifted away from our national steak-and-potato obsession. Now we can embrace the myriad healthful and interesting accompaniments to the simple grilled fish or chicken long enjoyed by countries where cattle barons never reigned. We can also accept that our recommended daily protein requirement doesn't have to be packed exclusively on our dinner plates.

Steamed farm-fresh vegetables, simply seasoned and lightly buttered, should always be prized, but such purist quality cannot often be duplicated. The sight of asparagus and corn on the cob in the market in January is seductive but seldom measures up. I'll save my veggie treats for the local farmers. You're welcome, Alice Waters.

Meanwhile, there are so many vegetable and grain side dishes that can be made ahead and don't have to leap from the ground to the pan to be nutritious or flavorful. They can add renewed interest to a meal of plain baked fish or grilled chicken. This chapter is only the beginning of the list of choices you have while waiting for the soil to bloom. A few recipes using grains, starches, or vegetables that can be reheated can become complete meals with the addition of a poached egg or a few ounces of cooked meat, poultry, seafood, or cheese. And, best of all, these recipes give you a good reason to return to the kitchen.

CANNELLINI SALAD with CELERY HEARTS and ROQUEFORT VINAIGRETTE

Serves 4 to 6

The mild flavor and creamy texture of the treasured bean of Tuscany is a perfect foil for an assertive cheese and crunchy celery. This salad stores well in the refrigerator and can easily be refreshed with an added drizzle of olive oil. It's a fine accompaniment to grilled meat or poultry and would make a complete and savory summer supper mounded on arugula and topped with a few slivers of cold rare steak. In mini-portions, it's palate-teasing enough to start off a company dinner cupped in a bright red leaf of radicchio.

1 pound dried cannellini beans, about
   2 cups
½ small onion stuck with 1 clove
1 carrot, cut in 3 pieces
Kosher salt and freshly ground
   black pepper
3 celery hearts, chopped
¼ cup minced flat-leaf parsley
¼ cup minced mint leaves

The Dressing:
4 garlic cloves, roasted
5 tablespoons extra-virgin olive oil
1 teaspoon Dijon mustard
1½ tablespoons lemon juice
1½ tablespoons red wine vinegar
½ cup crumbled Roquefort or other
   quality creamy blue cheese
1 tablespoon heavy cream (optional)

Rinse the beans and put them in a large pot with the onion and carrot covered by 3 inches of water. Bring them to a simmer and cook, covered, for an hour or more until they're tender but not mushy. Old beans take longer to cook. Remove the onion and carrot, drain, and allow the beans to cool to room temperature. Add salt and pepper to taste. Toss in the celery and herbs.

Mash the roasted garlic into a paste with some of the olive oil and place the mixture in a screw-top jar. Add the remaining oil and the rest of the ingredients and shake to combine. Pour half of the dressing over the beans and set them aside for an hour or more to marinate.

Taste for seasoning and add enough more dressing to make the salad glisten. It need not be refrigerated until several hours later.

COOK'S NOTES: *If possible, I recommend mixing the cream into the dressing. It pulls all the flavors together with the cheese.*

EAST INDIAN VEGETABLE SLAW

Serves 4

I keep forgetting about coleslaw, even though it's so wonderfully refreshing, satisfying, and good for you. This slaw will keep several days in the refrigerator, but I doubt it will last that long.

2 cups finely shredded green and/or cabbage

2 cups grated carrots and green and/or yellow squash, squeezed very dry

1 cup frozen baby peas, thawed and blotted

6 scallions, with ½ inch of the green, finely chopped

¼ to ⅓ cup currants (your preference)

¼ cup yogurt or sour cream

¼ cup mayonnaise, preferably Hellmann's or Best Foods (regular or light)

½ teaspoon Curry Powder (page 123)

1 teaspoon grated gingerroot

½ teaspoon dry mustard

½ teaspoon kosher salt, or to taste

Freshly ground black pepper

⅓ cup dry roasted peanuts for garnish (optional)

 Toss the vegetables and currants to combine. Whisk together the yogurt, mayonnaise, Curry Powder, ginger, and dry mustard. Toss the dressing into the vegetables. Taste and add salt and pepper. Garnish, if desired, with the peanuts.

COOK'S NOTES: *Grate the carrots and zucchini on the largest holes of a box grater. Be sure to squeeze most of the moisture from the zucchini with paper towels, or the dressing will water down. Lay the peas out on paper towels to thaw.*

If you like more zip in the salad, add a pinch of cayenne pepper or a dash of hot sauce to the dressing.

SWEET PINEAPPLE and CUCUMBER SALAD with DAIKON

Serves 4

The Dole pineapples tagged "extra sweet" taste just like the ones you get in Hawaii. This is a quirky salad with a lot of personality. It teams up well with teriyaki-glazed spareribs, grilled salmon, swordfish, or lamb. In case you're unfamiliar with daikon, it's that enormous white Japanese radish usually sold already cut in manageable chunks. It's zesty and delicious without the burn of our large red ones.

1½ cups slivered fresh pineapple
1½ cups chopped seeded cucumber
1 cup grated daikon
½ cup chopped red onion
¼ cup minced cilantro

1 teaspoon minced red chili
⅓ cup rice wine vinegar
1½ tablespoons water
2 tablespoons sugar

Combine the pineapple, cucumber, daikon, onion, cilantro, and chili. Combine the vinegar, water, and sugar in a screw-top jar and shake well. Add the dressing to the salad slowly, tasting as you go to achieve a pleasing sweet, sour, hot balance of flavors.

CHICKPEAS and SERRANO PEPPERS

Serves 4

This spicy salad is a welcome accompaniment for any hot or cold meat, poultry, or fish that needs a little culinary kick in the pants. You could add chopped hard-boiled eggs to it for a nice luncheon main course or warm the chickpeas and top them with a softly poached egg.

One 19-ounce can chickpeas, rinsed and drained

3 fresh tomatoes, seeded, pulped, and diced, or one 14½-ounce can diced, preferably Muir Glen, drained

½ cup chopped red onion

⅓ cup minced cilantro and/or parsley

1 serrano pepper or 2 small jalapeño peppers, or ½ habañero pepper, minced

The Dressing:

5 tablespoons extra-virgin olive oil

3 tablespoons lemon juice

3 garlic cloves, smashed and minced

½ teaspoon ground cumin

1 teaspoon kosher salt

Freshly ground black pepper

Toss together the chickpeas, tomatoes, onion, cilantro, and chili pepper(s). Shake the dressing ingredients in a screw-top jar and pour over the salad. Add the salt and pepper to taste.

WHEN TOMATOES ABOUND

Stewed tomatoes are simply delicious—both hot and cold. When there are more local, picture-perfect, vine-ripened tomatoes in the marketplace than you know what to do with, peel and core 6 to 8 big juicy ones. Leave them whole and put them in an enameled Dutch oven or other nonreactive pan with 2 to 3 tablespoons butter. Cover and cook for 1½ hours. Add 1½ tablespoons sugar and several gratings of nutmeg and cook another 30 minutes. Salt and pepper to taste.

RED CABBAGE and GREEN APPLE SALAD
with DILL VINAIGRETTE

This is another salad that looks pretty, tastes great, and teams up with most anything, particularly pork or fried Country-Style Sausage (page 80)—without the rosemary.

8 ounces red cabbage, finely shredded,
    about 4 cups
2 Granny Smith apples, unpeeled
    and grated
2/3 cup minced red onion
2 teaspoons Dijon honey mustard
3 tablespoons safflower oil

2 tablespoons walnut oil
3 tablespoons lemon juice
Pinch of sugar
1/4 cup minced fresh dill
Kosher salt and freshly ground
    black pepper

Combine the cabbage, grated apple, and onion. Put the remaining ingredients in a screw-top jar, shake well, and pour over the salad. Adjust the seasoning to taste and toss.

ROASTED ROOT VEGETABLES

Serves 6

*S*omething very close to this is served under grilled salmon at the Sea Grill restaurant in New York's Rockefeller Center, so I'm sad to say I can't take full credit. Actually, it's a gussied-up version of the classic British Bubble and Squeak, which began as a way to use up Sunday leftovers. When I made it in my kitchen I sampled right through my portion before the serving dish made it to the dinner table. It's surprising that a rather ordinary group of root vegetables can taste so extraordinary just because they're caramelized. Even more surprising is that they taste almost as good cold!

6 strips of smoked bacon, slivered
2 parsnips, peeled and cut in large chunks
3 carrots, peeled and quartered
2 Yukon Gold potatoes, peeled and quartered
1 fennel bulb, trimmed and quartered
2 white turnips, peeled and halved

1 sweet onion, peeled and quartered
8 garlic cloves, peeled and left whole
Olive oil for drizzling
Kosher salt and freshly ground black pepper
2 tablespoons fresh thyme leaves
2 tablespoons minced flat-leaf parsley

Preheat the oven to 475°. Put the bacon in a large roasting pan and render it on top of the stove until most of the fat drains but the bacon is not crisp. Remove it and chop it roughly. Spread all the vegetables in the pan in a single layer and toss them around in the bacon drippings. Pour off any excess. Add the bacon. Drizzle some olive oil over the top until everything glistens. Salt and pepper the mixture and toss in the thyme. Bake for 40 minutes, until the vegetables are well caramelized and a deep golden brown. Set aside until cool enough to handle.

With a large mixing bowl at hand to hold them, cut each of the vegetables into small dice and toss with the parsley. Taste for seasoning. Serve immediately or store and reheat.

COOK'S NOTES: *While preparing this dish, you may question the necessity of dicing the vegetables. When you take some on your fork, however, you'll see that it's the variety of flavors hitting your palate at once that makes this recipe special.*

ARTICHOKE HEARTS and CELERIAC in LEMON-CAPER SAUCE

Serves 4

The quickest way to serve artichokes is to snip off their needle-tipped leaves, plunge them into boiling water until tender, and pluck, dip, and eat. But without much more time and labor, you can remove the choke, stuff the base, and bake it. How long has it been since you've leisurely rounded multiple artichoke bottoms and stored them for any one of the divine dishes in which they might star? Preparing artichokes is an opportunity to lay hands on the food and marvel at the complexity of nature's design.

In spring and summer when the artichokes are piled high in the market and the price is right, consider stocking up. When properly prepared, they can be stored for days and can even be successfully frozen in olive oil. The commercially frozen ones pale in comparison.

6 medium artichokes, unblemished and heavy for their size	Lemon-Caper Sauce:
2 wedges of lemon	2 egg yolks
1 medium celery root (celeriac)	2 tablespoons lemon juice
1¼ cups homemade Chicken Broth (page 4) or Vegetable Broth (page 8)	Kosher salt and freshly ground black pepper
	1 tablespoon capers

❧ Fill a large mixing bowl with water and acidulate it with the juice of a fat lemon wedge, tossing in the squeezed rind as well. Cut off the stems of the artichokes so that they are even with the base. If the stems are at least 2 inches long and look plump and fresh, peel off the tough fibrous outer skin and slice them into ½-inch-thick circles. Drop them into the bowl.

With a serrated knife, cut off the top third of the artichoke and discard. Starting at the bottom, snap off the leaves, tipping them back and pulling straight down on each one, not out. When you get down to pale green and yellow leaves, cut across the remaining ones just above the level of the choke. Pull out the cap of pale prickly leaves over the choke, which can be most easily removed with a melon baller or a small sharp-edged spoon. Once every strand of fuzzy choke has been discarded, use a sharp paring knife to cut around the heart and its base, removing all traces of fibrous green. Drop each heart immediately into the acidulated water.

Trim and peel the celeriac and slice it about ¼ inch thick. Cut the circles into small wedges like a pie or cut them into ¼-inch batons, discarding the outside round edges. Drop them immediately into the acidulated water.

Bring a saucepanful of water to a boil, add the drained artichoke hearts, and simmer for about 10 minutes or until they pierce easily with the tip of a paring knife. Lift them out with a slotted spoon or flat sieve, cut in quarters, and set aside. Drain the water from the pan and add the broth. Bring it to a boil and add the drained celeriac. Reduce the heat, cover the pan, and simmer until tender, about 25 minutes. Lift the celeriac pieces from the broth with a slotted spoon and add them to the reserved hearts. Return the broth to the heat.

To make the sauce: Whisk the egg yolks with the lemon juice and temper them with some of the hot broth. Whisk the mixture vigorously into the gently simmering broth, pulling the pan on and off the heat to prevent the egg from scrambling. When the sauce has thickened, add the salt and pepper and capers and return the artichokes and celeriac to the pot to reheat. Serve immediately.

COOK'S NOTES: *To prepare this dish in stages, cook the artichokes and celeriac separately. When you are ready to serve the dish, reheat the broth. Make the Lemon-Caper Sauce and reheat the vegetables in it.*

COOKING AND STORING ARTICHOKE HEARTS

Trim and round 3 to 4 hearts, but leave the choke intact. In a large saucepan, whisk 2 tablespoons flour into 1 cup water until smooth. Add another cup of water, 1 tablespoon lemon juice, and a teaspoon of salt. Bring to a boil and simmer for 3 minutes, then reheat to boiling and submerge the hearts. Simmer for 20 to 30 minutes or until the hearts are tender. Cool in the liquid and refrigerate with a film of oil covering the liquid. Remove the chokes just before stuffing the hearts.

RED CABBAGE with SHALLOTS and DRIED CHERRIES

Serves 4 to 6

This recipe for a sweet-sour red cabbage was created when I was looking for a different way to serve the duck legs confit in the back of my fridge. Two full legs, vacuum-sealed by D'Artagnan, and available in specialty food stores, are reasonably priced and they're a dandy treat to have stored in your refrigerator. They keep, unopened, for weeks. The cabbage, duck confit, and steamed new potatoes make a satisfying supper. (See Cook's Notes to serve this recipe with duck.)

Another good suggestion for serving this cabbage is to team it with spicy homemade bulk sausage (page 80).

½ cup dried cherries

4 slices of smoked bacon, slivered

12 shallots or red pearl onions, peeled

½ head of red cabbage, cored and sliced about ¼ inch thick

¼ cup cider vinegar

½ teaspoon ground allspice

Kosher salt and freshly ground black pepper

3 tablespoons red currant jelly

Cover the cherries with water and let them soak for 20 minutes.

Place the slivered bacon in a deep sauté pan and render most of the fat over medium-high heat. Lower the heat, add the shallots, and sauté them until they are golden on the outside and still firm in the center.

Fluff out the cabbage into a colander and rinse it with cool water. Lift it into the sauté pan without shaking it dry. Cook over medium heat, tossing with tongs, until the cabbage wilts. Add the vinegar and allspice, cover the pan, and cook for about 20 minutes or until the cabbage is soft. If any liquid remains, remove the lid and allow it to evaporate until the cabbage is just moist. Add the salt, pepper, and the currant jelly. Toss to combine. The cabbage will be brightly glazed. Taste for seasoning until you get a pleasing balance of sweet and sour. Don't under-salt.

COOK'S NOTES: *If you want to try this cabbage with the duck confit, omit the bacon and brown the duck legs to release as much fat from the surface as you can. Remove the legs to a cutting board and continue with the recipe. When the duck is cool, pull off the meat in chunks and add to the finished cabbage. There's little fat on the duck confit, but duck fat in jars is also available in specialty food stores. It keeps best in the freezer. Use a little duck fat to replace the bacon fat in this recipe, and use it to sauté or roast the accompanying potatoes.*

EGGPLANT RAGOUT

Serves 4 to 6

Although this dish couldn't be a better all-in-one partner *for any simply prepared meat, chicken, or fish, my favorite way to serve this ragout is dusted with grated Parmigiano-Reggiano, a poached egg perched on top, and crisscrossed with anchovy fillets. It's such a quick and delicious brunch or supper dish when you have the ragout waiting in the fridge.*

¼ cup extra-virgin olive oil

3 firm, shiny Italian eggplants, peeled and cubed, about 4 cups

½ medium red onion, chopped

3 garlic cloves, smashed and minced

Dried red pepper flakes to taste

½ red bell pepper and ½ yellow bell pepper, julienned

½ teaspoon dried thyme

Kosher salt and freshly ground black pepper

One 14½-ounce can diced tomatoes, drained, preferably Muir Glen

¼ cup minced flat-leaf parsley

¼ cup slivered mint or basil leaves

4 small red potatoes, sliced

Water or homemade Vegetable Broth (page 8)

Heat the oil in a large, lidded sauté pan and sauté the eggplant, onion, garlic, pepper flakes, bell peppers, thyme, salt, and pepper until the eggplant is tender. If necessary, add more oil to prevent the mixture from sticking. (You can pour off any excess oil after the eggplant is done.)

Add the tomatoes, parsley, mint, and potatoes and combine. Pour in enough water or broth to cover the mixture a third of the way up. Cover the pan and simmer for 20 minutes or until the potatoes are tender. Check the liquid level halfway through to make sure the ragout isn't dry. It should be loose and moist but not watery. If necessary, evaporate any excess liquid with the lid off. Serve immediately or store and reheat.

COOK'S NOTES: *Yet another wonderful way to turn this ragout into a small supper or a more substantial side dish is to add diced fresh mozzarella to the mixture when you reheat it. You cannot, however, reheat with the mozzarella already melted in it or the cheese will be rubbery.*

A delicious and protein-rich alternative to the potato is to stir in cooked cannellini beans instead. The mozzarella is also welcome in this case.

ROASTED CHILI and CORN BREAD PUDDING

Serves 6

*S*ince *I always buy artisanal bakery bread* and never seem to finish it, stale bread is too often around. Savory bread puddings are the answer, and they're so tasty and satisfying that I now buy great bread without guilt and sometimes just for this purpose.

I've tried this cheese-custard base with caramelized onion and strips of tomato; three-color roasted bell peppers; and sautéed fennel and Kalamata olives. I've served it with grilled fish, rotisserie chicken, and garlicky sautéed shrimp. The possibilities go on.

4 to 6 roasted mixed peppers, such
    as poblano, pasilla, Anaheim,
    New Mexico, or jalapeño, peeled
2 tablespoons butter
1/2 cup minced onion
1 cup corn kernels, fresh or frozen,
    thawed (optional)
1 teaspoon kosher salt

Freshly ground black pepper
4 eggs
3 cups whole milk
1 1/2 cups grated Monterey Jack or
    Cheddar cheese
About 1/2 loaf rustic bakery bread,
    in rough chunks, 4 cups

❧ Pull the stems from the peeled peppers and remove the seeds. Tear the peppers into fat strips.

Heat the butter in a small skillet and briefly sauté the onion. If the corn was frozen, blot it dry on paper towels. Add the fresh or frozen kernels to the onion and sauté over medium-high heat until the mixture starts to caramelize, picking up golden brown flecks. Add the salt and pepper.

Whisk the eggs and combine with the milk. Stir in the corn and onion mixture along with the chili strips and the cheese.

Put the bread in a large mixing bowl and pour the chili custard over it. Toss well to combine all the ingredients. Allow the pudding to sit for 30 minutes.

Preheat the oven to 350°.

Butter a 2-quart casserole dish and fill it with the pudding, checking to make sure everything is distributed evenly. Bake for 1 hour. When the pudding is done, it will have pulled away from the sides of the casserole and the center will be firm. Serve, or store to reheat.

COOK'S NOTES: *You can also bake this pudding in individual ramekins in a roasting pan filled halfway up with boiling water. Bake for 30 to 45 minutes or until the pudding has pulled away from the sides of the dishes and the centers are firm. Unmold onto a heated platter garnished with a sprinkling of chopped herbs for a tasty addition to a casual buffet.*

ARUGULA GNOCCHI

Serves 4

Gnocchi made with ricotta cheese instead of the traditional potato are called naked ravioli (*ravioli nudi*), a whimsical example of the affection Italians seem to have for their food. Whatever they're called, these little dumplings are delicate and versatile. They can be made with spinach or Swiss chard or simply basil and parsley. The ricotta can be mixed with a little Gorgonzola or sautéed minced porcini. They can be sauced with brown butter and fennel, buttered peas and prosciutto, fresh tomato sauce with slivered artichoke hearts, or sage garlic butter and Parmesan cheese. They couldn't be easier to make and, once poached, they store well.

3 large bunches of arugula, about
    1½ pounds
12 ounces fresh ricotta, well drained in
    the refrigerator, preferably overnight
3 eggs, beaten
½ cup flour

½ cup freshly grated Parmigiano-
    Reggiano
Freshly grated nutmeg
Kosher salt and freshly ground
    black pepper

Cut off the roots and stems of the arugula. Rinse the leaves under running water and then float them in a sink full of water to release every speck of sandy soil. Bring a stockpot of salted water to a boil and blanch the arugula for 3 minutes. Drain in a colander, squeeze the leaves very dry, and then blot with paper towels. Measure out 1½ cups of arugula, chop very fine, and pick out any remaining fat stems. Blot the arugula again with paper towels and blot any excess liquid from the ricotta as well.

Refill the pot with water and bring it to a gentle simmer. Combine all the ingredients and with moist hands form cork-shaped cylinders. Poach the gnocchi, a few at a time, until they rise to the top, about 5 to 8 minutes. Do not allow the water to boil. Carefully remove the gnocchi to a colander with a slotted spoon.

Serve with a light *beciamella* sauce (see Cook's Notes) and grated Parmigiano-Reggiano, or cover and store in the refrigerator plain. To reheat, place the gnocchi single-file in a gratin dish, nap them with the sauce, and bake in a moderate oven until piping hot.

COOK'S NOTES: *Like spinach, arugula seems to dissolve into the cooking water. One half pound of fresh arugula renders less than 1 cup cooked and dried, so one and a half pounds isn't overkill. Therefore, these gnocchi are more affordable when arugula is plentiful (late spring through late summer) and shows up in the market in fat bunches.*

To make the béchamel sauce: Heat 2 tablespoons butter in a small saucepan, whisking in

1 tablespoon flour. Add kosher salt and freshly ground black pepper and a pinch of cayenne. Whisking vigorously, slowly add a cup of hot milk, half and half, or cream and simmer until the sauce lightly thickens. Add ¼ cup grated Parmigiano-Reggiano and pour the sauce over the gnocchi. The sauce will thicken further as it bakes.

For a quicker serve, simply drizzle the gnocchi with browned butter, sprinkle with Parmigiano-Reggiano, and bake. Toasted pine nuts are a nice garnish.

KEEPER PUREES

Cauliflower: Steam in the microwave in milk until very tender. Place in a blender with a knob of butter, salt, pepper, and some of the milk, adding more milk as needed. Puree until the cauliflower is fluffy and as creamy as mashed potatoes. Store, and reheat in the microwave.

Broccoli: Steam in the microwave with water or vegetable broth. Proceed as above, adding some Roasted Garlic (page 155). Reheat in the oven topped with buttered bread crumbs and grated Parmigiano-Reggiano.

Cannellini Beans: Simmer 1 cup cannellini beans with a single sprig of rosemary, half an onion, and 2 whole garlic cloves. They should be tender in 2 hours if they haven't been soaked—30 to 40 minutes if they have. Drain and remove the rosemary and onion. Puree the beans with the garlic, 3 tablespoons olive oil, 2 tablespoons lemon juice, salt, and pepper. Reheat in the microwave.

HERBED SWEET POTATO and CELERIAC GRATIN

In this recipe, celery root offers a savory contrast to the natural sweetness of the potato, and the herbed cream gently bridges the flavor gap. This gratin goes well with most anything but, of course, is particularly special with ham, pork roast, or your holiday turkey.

3 sweet potatoes, peeled

1 medium celeriac, trimmed and peeled

Kosher salt and freshly ground black pepper

1/3 cup grated Parmigiano-Reggiano, plus more for topping

1/4 cup minced flat-leaf parsley, chives, and chervil

1 cup heavy cream

Pinch of cayenne pepper

Grated nutmeg

Preheat the oven to 350°. Butter a flameproof gratin dish.

Slice the potatoes and celeriac very thin on a mandoline or any other slicing gadget. Fill the dish with overlapping layers of potatoes and celeriac, seasoning each layer with salt and pepper and a sprinkling of the cheese, parsley, chives, and chervil.

Season the cream with cayenne and nutmeg and pour it over the potatoes. Bring the gratin to a simmer on top of the stove and let it cook for 5 minutes before topping it with more cheese and sliding it into the oven. Bake for about 30 to 45 minutes or until a sharp knife pierces the celeriac easily.

GARLICKY POTATO WEDGES

Steam potatoes, preferably Yukon Golds, in the microwave until just tender. Whisk up a vinaigrette dressing with Dijon mustard, lemon juice, olive oil, fresh thyme leaves, and lots of smashed, minced garlic. Cut the warm potatoes into wedges, dress them with the vinaigrette, and let them cool to room temperature. Refrigerate up to 4 days and then bake at 450° until crispy. Salt and pepper.

GOLD POTATOES BRAISED in BUTTERMILK and DILL

Serves 4 to 6

Yukon Gold potatoes taste so distinctly rich and creamy that their character shines through this low-fat braise in buttermilk and dill. You might want to double the recipe and use the leftovers as a delicious base for potato salad.

6 Yukon Gold potatoes, peeled and diced
2½ cups buttermilk
Kosher salt and freshly ground
    black pepper

⅓ cup minced dill
2 tablespoons snipped chives
2 tablespoons minced flat-leaf parsley

Use a heavy-bottomed pan or an enameled Dutch oven. Simmer the potatoes in the buttermilk, seasoned with salt and pepper, over very low heat. Cook until the milk is absorbed and the potatoes are tender. Add the herbs at the halfway point and toss to combine. Serve or store.

TWICE-BAKED POTATOES

Always bake extra potatoes and refrigerate. Chop them roughly, with or without the skins. Melt canola oil and butter in a skillet with an ovenproof handle and cook them over medium-high heat until the bottom is brown. Season with salt, freshly ground black pepper, and a touch of freshly grated nutmeg. Dot with butter and put the skillet in a 450° oven to finish browning. Grate Gruyère cheese over the top and quickly melt under the broiler, or serve with yogurt and/or sour cream and chives.

POLENTA with GORGONZOLA and CARAMELIZED ONIONS

There's nothing more comforting than a mound of buttery-soft polenta. This delicious alternative seems born to accompany a juicy grilled strip steak, and you can make it ahead. I see no reason not to use the Italian imported Polenta Express, which, according to the amusing instructions on the box, can be made in the microwave in twice the time!

1 quart water, vegetable broth, or chicken broth

2 teaspoons kosher salt

1 cup instant polenta

8 ounces crumbled Gorgonzola or Maytag Blue

1 cup toasted chopped walnuts

1½ cups Caramelized Onions (page 126)

 Preheat the oven to 350°. Butter a 9-inch springform pan, quiche pan, or shallow round casserole.

Bring the water or broth to a rolling boil in a saucepan and add the salt. Reduce the heat to medium and very slowly pour in the polenta, stirring constantly with a wooden spoon. (Hold your face away from the pan. Polenta can bubble up and jettison extremely hot bits.) In about 5 minutes the polenta will have thickened and pulled away from the sides of the pan. Remove it from the heat and pour half the mixture into the prepared pan. Smooth it out with a spatula.

Sprinkle the first layer with half the cheese, walnuts, and onions. Cover with the rest of the polenta and top with the remaining cheese, nuts, and onions.

To serve, bake for 30 minutes and cut into wedges, or allow to cool, cover, and store for baking later.

SAFFRON RICE PILAF

Serves 6

good dinner is assured if there's leftover rice in the fridge. A properly cooked pilaf can be gently reheated, and cold boiled rice can climb to greater glory in the guise of a shrimp and vegetable–studded fried rice. This recipe produces an aromatic, vaguely sweet East Indian pilaf that begs to be served with spicy lamb, chicken, or duck. It would also make a lovely stuffing, bound with a beaten egg, and a stunning companion to some of that leftover holiday turkey.

1/2 teaspoon crumbled saffron threads
1/2 cup hot water
3 tablespoons unsalted butter
3 shallots, minced
One 2-inch piece of cinnamon stick
6 green cardamom pods
6 whole cloves

1 1/2 cups basmati rice
3 tablespoons currants or chopped dried
  apricots
3 tablespoons sugar
2 1/2 cups Chicken Broth (page 4), homemade or low-sodium canned
1 teaspoon kosher salt

 Set the saffron aside to dissolve in the hot water. Melt the butter in a heavy-bottomed sauté pan with a tight-fitting lid or in an enameled iron Dutch oven. Add the shallots and spices and sauté just until the shallots soften and the spices release their perfume.

Add the rice and stir to coat the grains with the spicy butter. Cook over medium-high heat until the rice is translucent, stirring constantly. Add the currants, sugar, broth, and salt. Bring the broth to a simmer and turn the heat down to the lowest setting. Set the pan on a flame tamer, cover with the lid, and allow the rice to cook undisturbed for 20 minutes. Remove the lid to check the rice. It should be dry with little steam craters on the surface. Replace the lid and let the rice sit off the heat for 5 minutes. Fluff with a fork and serve, or allow to cool and then store in the refrigerator.

COOK'S NOTES: *Pilaf reheats well in a 350° oven spread out in a 1-inch layer on a baking dish.*

BAKED RED and GREEN RICE PILAF

Serves 4

This piquant pilaf illustrates two departures from the classic preparation. First of all, the flavors are folded in after the rice has been sautéed in the oil, and second, it's baked. Baking the rice has two advantages: It keeps the stove top free, and the even temperature of the oven encourages better water absorption. Unless you're very familiar with the absorption properties of the rice you use, achieving the perfect separate grains can be tricky.

This recipe adapts to many variations. You could fold in roasted green chilies; the typical Mexican peas and carrots; black beans; avocado cubes; fried plantains; raisins and hulled pumpkin seeds (*pepitas*); or slivers of fresh pineapple.

2 tablespoons safflower oil, canola oil, or lard

3 tablespoons chopped onion

1 garlic clove, smashed and minced

1½ cups long-grain white rice (not converted)

2½ cups Chicken Broth (page 4), homemade or low-sodium canned

Kosher salt and freshly ground black pepper

4 fresh plum tomatoes, peeled, pulped, and slivered

1 tablespoon minced pickled jalapeños (optional)

½ cup chopped parsley

⅓ cup chopped cilantro, for garnish

❧ Preheat the oven to 350°.

Heat the oil in an ovenproof lidded dish or in a sauté pan with a metal handle. Add the onion, garlic, and rice and cook, stirring, until the onion is soft and the rice translucent and lightly golden. Pour in the broth and salt and pepper lightly. Add the tomatoes, jalapeños, and parsley. Cover and bake until the rice is tender, about 25 minutes. Remove from the oven and let stand, covered, for 5 minutes.

Sprinkle the top with the cilantro and fork it through the rice.

COOK'S NOTES: *The pilaf will keep for 3 days in the refrigerator and can be reheated.*

MINTED COUSCOUS with MEDJOOL DATES and PRESERVED LEMON

Serves 4

Aficionados of the traditional method of cooking couscous, who might disdain the use of the quick variety, should feel free to do it the laborious way. But this recipe is more reminiscent than authentic, so I'll skip my apologies to Paula Wolfert, the master of Moroccan cuisine.

This is a delicious side dish for grilled lamb.

4 tablespoons (½ stick) butter
½ cup chopped sweet onion
1½ teaspoons grated gingerroot
½ teaspoon cinnamon
¼ teaspoon turmeric
1¼ cups Chicken Broth (page 4), homemade or low-sodium canned

¼ cup chopped Medjool dates
1 tablespoon minced Preserved Lemons (page 125) or lemon juice
¼ cup chopped mint leaves
1 cup quick couscous
Kosher salt and freshly ground black pepper

Melt the butter in a deep, lidded sauté pan. Add the onion and ginger and cook, covered, over medium-low heat for about 15 minutes, until the onion is soft but not brown. Add the cinnamon and turmeric and stir to combine.

Add the broth, dates, lemon, and mint and bring to a simmer. Stir in the couscous and cover the pan. Let the mixture stand for about 10 minutes or until all the liquid is absorbed. Fluff the couscous with a fork and season to taste.

WEST INDIAN RED BEANS

Serves 6

If you have a proper bean pot, you might want to double this recipe and freeze half of it. Beans freeze very well and are a great addition to the larder, since they make such a wonderful side dish for almost any main course. I even like these beans cold.

1 pound pinto or kidney beans
One 4-ounce piece of salt pork
4 whole cloves
1 medium onion, quartered
4 garlic cloves, chopped
3 quarter-size slices of ginger, slivered
4 plum tomatoes, peeled, seeded,
   and chopped

1 Scotch bonnet (or habañero) pepper,
   seeded and minced
1/3 cup light molasses
2 cups Chicken Broth (page 4),
   homemade or low-sodium canned
Kosher salt and freshly ground
   black pepper

Rinse the beans, picking out any stones or debris. Cover with cool water and allow to soak 6 hours or overnight.

Preheat the oven to 250°.

Cut the salt pork in half and score it down to the rind in several places. Insert the cloves in the uncut side of the onion quarters. Put half the pork, onion, garlic, ginger, tomatoes, and chili pepper in the bottom of a narrow-neck bean pot or a deep-lidded casserole. Pour half the beans on top and add the remaining seasonings. Add the rest of the beans. Pour the molasses and broth over the top and fill the pot with water to just under the level of the beans. Cover the pot and bake for 4 to 6 hours. Check the progress regularly to make certain that the water level remains constant. Add the salt and pepper no less than halfway through the baking.

COOK'S NOTES: *Even after the beans are cooked, they may seem too soupy. As they cool, they'll absorb a good deal of the cooking broth, so don't attempt to drain or evaporate the excess broth. Baked beans are better after they've been stored and their flavors have mingled. They will keep at least a week in the refrigerator, freeze perfectly, and reheat easily.*

CONDIMENTS, SALSAS, and SAUCES

5

The more complex sauces of classic French cuisine will never lose their power to seduce, but their preeminence has waned as the pace of our lives has quickened. Our priorities shifted and we sought lighter fare. Following the trend, inventive chefs everywhere showed us simpler ways to garnish a meal. Their creative curiosity about unfamiliar cuisines and their collaboration with foreign colleagues has enriched our own cuisine and reminded us again that it's so often the little things that count.

Condiments, salsas, relishes, savory marmalades, confits—their differences are blurred and their names are increasingly meaningless and interchangeable. Condiments are commonly defined as preserved sideline accents, like pickles, mustards, and chutneys, which can spark up an otherwise dull meal. The term can also encompass flavor-enhancing seasonings and extracts. They're the ultimate keepers.

I like the Spanish word *salsa*—it trips easily off the tongue and is gaily onomatopoetic. Its origin blurred, it has become a culinary buzzword. In the current lexicon, hot or cold salsas are bright and savory, encompassing an unlimited range of vegetables, fruits, and herbs. Best of all, there are no rules for making or inventing them except that they remain chunky, moist, and preferably uncooked. Mexican salsas usually contain chilies, but professional chefs, using a more international interpretation, present them sweet, hot, or both, and use them under, over, or alongside the food they garnish. They enhance, complement, and transform a simple meal. Although more integral to the dish they accompany, salsas are sometimes hard to distinguish from condiments.

Sauces are defined as liquids, but I can think of many that are more like salsas. There are several light sauces, including ethnic and pasta sauces, in this chapter because they can be made ahead, refrigerated for several days, or frozen, which is what weekend cooking is all about.

At the beginning of the chapter I list a handy hodgepodge of compound butters, flavored mayonnaise, curry powder and paste, toppings, and dips that defy logical categorizing but are wildly useful to have on hand.

COMPOUND BUTTERS

*C*ompound butters are the simplest embellishments *for meat, fish, and poultry alike. Store them in crocks in the fridge, freeze them in ice-cube tray portions or in bricks that you can slice with a butter curler or vegetable peeler. Be sure to label the plastic bag they're stored in, for you'll quickly forget which herb is which.

The seasoning is the star, not the butter. Use only enough butter to solidify the mixture. Compound butter is not about drowning an otherwise lean chop or fish fillet in fat. Rather, a small pat will vastly improve the flavor, and smearing a little under the skin of a chicken or Cornish hen will accent and complement the bird.

All of these compound butters can be made quickly in the food processor with slightly softened butter, or they can be mixed by hand. You can also make them in small portions just before serving, whenever you're in need of an instant sauce.

By food processor: In the bowl of a food processor, combine the butter, cut into pieces, and the seasonings. Pulse until well blended. Pack into a bowl or shape into a log and refrigerate, tightly wrapped in plastic wrap, until ready to use.

By hand: In a bowl, cream together the softened butter and the seasoning.

ANCHOVY BUTTER

1 stick unsalted butter, 4 to 6 anchovies, 2 roasted garlic cloves, ¼ cup chopped parsley, pinch of dried red pepper flakes.

OLIVE BUTTER WITH ROSEMARY AND GARLIC

1 stick unsalted butter, 1½ teaspoons dried rosemary, 1 teaspoon smashed and minced garlic, 2 tablespoons chopped Kalamata olives. *Note:* Sauté the garlic and rosemary in a pat of butter before combining them with the other ingredients.

JALAPEÑO CILANTRO BUTTER

1 stick unsalted butter, ½ seeded minced jalapeño pepper, 1 tablespoon minced cilantro, 1 tablespoon minced flat-leaf parsley. *Note:* Sauté the chili in a pat of butter before combining it with the other ingredients.

LEMON-THYME BUTTER

1 stick unsalted butter, 1½ tablespoons thyme leaves, 1 tablespoon minced flat-leaf parsley, 1 teaspoon grated lemon zest, salt, pepper.

SPICY GINGER-LIME BUTTER

1 stick unsalted butter, 1 teaspoon grated gingerroot, ½ teaspoon grated lime zest, ¼ teaspoon cayenne pepper.

ORANGE-CURRY BUTTER

1 stick unsalted butter; 1 shallot, minced; 1 garlic clove, smashed and minced; 1½ teaspoons Curry Powder; 2 teaspoons grated orange zest.
Note: Sauté the shallot, garlic, and curry powder in a pat of butter before combining it with the other ingredients.

MUSHROOM-SHERRY BUTTER

1 stick unsalted butter; 2 ounces minced rehydrated dried mushrooms, squeezed dry; 2 tablespoons minced flat-leaf parsley; ¼ teaspoon black pepper; salt; 1 tablespoon dry sherry.

HAZELNUT-ORANGE BUTTER

1 stick unsalted butter; ¼ cup toasted hazelnuts, finely chopped; 1 teaspoon grated orange zest.

ALMOND-CHEESE BUTTER

1 stick unsalted butter; ¼ cup toasted blanched almonds, finely chopped; 1 tablespoon minced chives; 2 tablespoons freshly grated Parmigiano-Reggiano; salt; freshly ground black pepper.

FLAVORED MAYONNAISE

There's little comparison between the classic French mayonnaise sauce and our beloved bottled salad dressing by the same name, and there are times when only the former will do. The blender or food processor allows for a foolproof mayonnaise, but unfortunately, homemade mayonnaise can't be safely stored for more than 4 or 5 days and it can't be frozen. The answer? Make homemade mayonnaise in small quantities when its silky texture and rich flavor are important, and keep boldly seasoned bottled mayonnaise on hand for spontaneous meal dress-ups.

Even homemade mayonnaise can be lightened if you've relegated it to the diet restricted list. (See suggestions below.) Mayonnaise and its derivative sauces are simply too versatile, quick, and delicious not to be enjoyed.

BLENDER MAYONNAISE

Blend 1 room temperature egg and 1 yolk on puree speed for several seconds with ½ teaspoon Dijon mustard and 1 teaspoon lemon juice. With the motor running, drizzle ¾ cup of safflower oil through the feed hole in the lid, pausing briefly to allow the sauce to absorb and thicken. If the mayonnaise reaches the desired consistency before all the oil has been added, stop. Scrape the sauce into a bowl and stir in another teaspoon of lemon juice. Season with salt and white pepper to taste. This should make about 1 cup.

CHANGING THE FLAVOR WITH OIL

Use half olive oil or one-third chili oil. Replace ¼ cup of the safflower oil with walnut or hazelnut oil. Add 3 to 4 drops of pure lime or orange oil, or replace 2 tablespoons of safflower oil with truffle oil or any seasoned oil of your choice. See page 155 for garlic and herb oils.

TO DOCTOR BOTTLED MAYONNAISE

Whisk ½ teaspoon Dijon mustard and 1 to 2 teaspoons lemon juice with 1 egg yolk and combine with 1 cup Hellmann's or Best Foods mayonnaise.

ADD-IN FLAVORS

Fold in ¼ cup minced green herbs such as cilantro, parsley, chives, basil, mint, tarragon, or chervil. Whisk in freshly grated horseradish or seasoned mustard to taste. Release the flavor of 2 teaspoons curry powder by heating for 2 minutes in 1 tablespoon of oil. Let the mixture cool before adding it to the mayonnaise.

TO LIGHTEN MAYONNAISE

Whisk in ⅓ cup low-fat yogurt or sour cream. You can also thin the sauce with another flavor dimension by whisking in pureed roasted red pepper, tomato puree, reduced broth, dry sherry, or *pastis*.

LEFTOVER BAKERY BREAD

Now that we can spend as much as $5.00 for a loaf of decent bread, having it perish before we can eat it up is disappointing. But there are a variety of ways to use leftover bread. Make croutons for soup or salad: Tear the bread into small chunks; toss it or spray it with olive oil and bake it at 325° until it's just firm and crispy, not hard. Croutons will store in a tightly sealed container for a long time.

If you have a lot of bread left over from a dinner party, make a savory Bread Pudding (page 104).

One thing you should never have to buy is bread crumbs. Slice the bread and let it dry out on a tray, or dry it in a slow oven. Process the dried bread into crumbs and store in screw-top containers.

SAUCE PARISIENNE with DILL

Makes about 1 cup

*T*his sauce, served over raw green and yellow zucchini, whole grape tomatoes, and slivered scallions accompanied by thick slices of cold garlicky roast lamb, was a runaway summer supper favorite at my restaurant.

8 ounces cream cheese or Neufchâtel, softened
½ teaspoon kosher salt
½ teaspoon paprika
Pinch of cayenne pepper

2 tablespoons lemon juice
½ cup safflower oil
White pepper to taste
3 tablespoons minced flat-leaf parsley
3 tablespoons minced dill

Place the cream cheese in the food processor and pulse to soften. Add the salt, paprika, cayenne, and lemon juice and combine. With the motor running, drizzle the oil through the feed tube and blend until you have a creamy emulsion. Taste for seasoning. Add white pepper and more lemon juice if needed, and then mix in the parsley and dill.

COOK'S NOTES: *Try this sauce in place of mayonnaise in potato salad.*

CURRY POWDER

Makes about ½ cup

Every Indian housewife has her own curry powder mixture. This one came from a good friend of mine who was married in India and became an accomplished Indian cook. I don't know whether this recipe came from her or from Julie Sahni, who became her friend and culinary mentor when she returned to New York. Whatever its origin, it's been my favorite for years.

2 tablespoons coriander seeds
1½ tablespoons cumin seeds
¾ teaspoon mustard seeds
¾ teaspoon fenugreek seeds
1 tablespoon ground cinnamon
2 tablespoons freshly ground
    black pepper

¾ teaspoon grated nutmeg
¾ teaspoon ground cloves
1½ teaspoons ground cardamom
1½ teaspoons turmeric
1½ teaspoons ground ginger
2 teaspoons to 1 tablespoon cayenne
    pepper (for mild to very hot curry)

Preheat the oven to 325°. Toast the seeds on a metal pie plate until the mustard seeds begin to pop. Be careful not to scorch them or the powder will be bitter. Cool. Process or blend the seeds with the rest of the ingredients. Store in a cool, dark place in a screw-top jar. Keeps for 3 to 4 months.

THAI GREEN CURRY PASTE

Makes about ½ cup

You can buy bottled Thai curry paste, but homemade has more vibrancy, and becoming familiar with the ingredients unveils some of the mysteries of Thai cooking. Sauté chicken or shrimp, add half of this paste, a couple of cups of Thai coconut milk, and a couple of tablespoons of *nam pla* (Thai fish sauce), and you have a memorable curry in less than 15 minutes. The paste will keep refrigerated for a month or can be frozen.

5 serrano peppers, stemmed, seeded, and minced

3 shallots, chopped

4 garlic cloves, chopped

4 quarter-size slices of ginger, chopped

2 teaspoons grated lime zest

1 lemongrass stalk, trimmed and minced, tender inside part only

2 flat anchovies, chopped

1 teaspoon ground coriander

1 teaspoon grated nutmeg

½ teaspoon ground cumin

½ teaspoon ground white pepper

¼ teaspoon ground cloves

½ teaspoon salt

¼ cup chopped cilantro with some of the stem or, preferably, the root

3 tablespoons peanut oil

Puree all the ingredients in the food processor, or pound to a paste using a mortar and pestle. Store in a screw-top jar.

PRESERVED LEMONS

I'm still finding uses for Preserved Lemons, although I was slow to include them in my pantry because I thought of them as exclusive to Moroccan cuisine. Curiosity prevailed, and a month later the necessity of using them inspired some very tasty inventions. Having real lemons at hand when I needed a touch of their tang has been a blessing. I've minced them into a parsley salad with a balsamic vinegar dressing; added them to Caesar salad and potato salad for a more lemony kick; tossed minced bits into brown butter to top fish fillets; and jazzed up a chicken stuffing. An added plus is their jarred beauty, which makes me think of Christmas gifts—maybe stacked alternately with limes.

One 20-ounce widemouthed glass jar or clamp-lock jar with rubber gasket
4 to 5 lemons, scrubbed in soapy water and rinsed
4 to 5 tablespoons kosher salt
1/2 cup freshly squeezed lemon juice

Run the jar through the dishwasher to be sure it's scrupulously clean.

You can place the lemons in the microwave on high for 2 minutes to release the juice from the pulp, or just roll them on the counter, pressing down hard.

Place the lemons over a bowl to catch the juice and cut them into quarters vertically from the stem end without cutting all the way through. Open the lemons up into four petals so they can be stacked over one another. Place the salt and lemon juice in the microwave, and bring it to a boil, dissolving the salt. *Note:* This will take from 2 to 3 minutes, depending on the wattage of the microwave. Do not let the lemon juice boil over.

Place one lemon on the bottom of the jar, pressing down with the back of a spoon to release most of the juice. Stack the remaining lemons in the same manner. Pour the salted lemon juice over the top. There should be enough to cover the lemons. If not, drizzle in a little more juice or water. Seal the jar and store in a cool, dark place for a month, turning the jar upside down once in a while for the first week.

To use the lemons, pull one out with tongs, not your fingers. Cut off a quarter or more, and return the rest to the jar. Pull out the pulp, if you like, and rinse the rind briefly under running water to remove any excess salt. Chop or mince, depending on use. The pickling juice can be reused many times.

COOK'S NOTES: *Preserved Lemons can also be made by just submerging the cut salted lemons in olive oil and keeping them sealed in a screw-top jar. As you use up the lemons, the excess oil is a wonderful addition to salad dressings—or it can even be used for sautéing fish.*

If you're going to use Preserved Lemons in various ways, this may be the preferred method of preserving them.

CARAMELIZED ONIONS

Makes 1 quart

Caramelized Onions take first prize for versatility for busy cooks, provided, of course, you're as fond of onions as I am. They take a bit of patience to make properly, but once they're done they keep for at least a week in the refrigerator and for longer in the freezer. My best advice is to double the recipe and pack them in widemouthed pint glass jars—some for the fridge, some for the freezer. After you see how much you can do with them, you'll consider the effort well worth it.

2 tablespoons butter
2 tablespoons olive oil
4 large white sweet onions, sliced

Kosher salt and freshly ground black
   pepper

Heat the butter and oil in a large, deep sauté pan with a lid. Add the onions and season. Turn the heat to its lowest level and use a heat diffuser if you have gas burners. Cover the pan and allow the onions to completely soften and become translucent. Do not lift the lid for the first 20 minutes. If, at that point, the onions are not quite soft and show no hint of browning, toss the onions, return the lid, and cook further, checking them at 10-minute intervals.

As soon as the onions are ready, remove the lid and raise the heat to start the caramelization process. To achieve a deep golden brown, another 20 minutes of cooking may be necessary.

You can use this mixture as a base for onion soup. Just add homemade broth, wine, croustades, and grated Gruyère. Pureed with chicken broth and a pinch of saffron, it also makes a delicious sauce for grilled chicken or fish.

VARIATION:

Sauté diced pancetta until crisp. Remove it to drain and use the fat to cook the onions. When they are caramelized, add balsamic vinegar and simmer to evaporate. Return the pancetta and serve over fish or veal chops.

USE CARAMELIZED ONIONS AS A TOPPING FOR:

▪ Pork or lamb chops, steak, hamburgers, grilled chicken, soft or grilled polenta with cheese, baked potato, pizza, focaccia, omelets

STIR-INS:

▪ roasted garlic, rosemary, and thyme (for lamb or veal)

▪ barbecue sauce (for grilled chicken, burgers, or pork)

▪ honey mustard and grated horseradish (for salmon)

▪ pomegranate molasses, crushed red pepper, and cilantro (for lamb or chicken)

▪ curry powder, yogurt, and cilantro (for chicken)

GARLIC MUSHROOMS with FRIZZLED PROSCIUTTO

Serves 4

I suppose this could be considered a side dish, but the addition of prosciutto changes its character. I prefer it as a topping for chicken or veal or as a brunch or light supper main dish over barley pilaf, grilled polenta, crostini with melted Fontina, challah Parmesan toast, risotto cakes, or a Gruyère cheese omelet. The reduction of some heavy cream with the mushrooms will make any one of these options even more luscious.

1 pound cremini mushrooms
2 tablespoons olive oil
1 tablespoon butter
2 garlic cloves, sliced
3 paper-thin slices prosciutto di Parma, slivered

¼ teaspoon dried thyme
2 tablespoons minced parsley
Kosher salt and freshly ground
    black pepper

Wipe the mushrooms with a damp paper towel and cut the stems even with the caps. Cut the mushrooms into quarters or eighths if they are large.

Melt the oil and butter in a large sauté pan. Add the garlic and sauté over low heat until the slices just start to turn golden. Remove them with a slotted spoon and discard, or save for another use. Pull the visible fat from the ham. Increase the heat, and shake the slivers loose into the oil. As soon as the ham frizzles but before it crisps, remove it with a slotted spoon and set it aside on paper towels to drain.

With the oil still hot, add the mushrooms and thyme. Sauté them quickly, tossing often to evaporate their juices. When the mushrooms are golden, remove them from the heat and stir in the parsley. Season with salt and pepper, but be cautious with salt as the prosciutto is salty. The mushrooms can be stored for several days and reheated. Freezing is not recommended.

ASIAN PEANUT SAUCE

Makes 2 cups

I'm certain our childhood love of peanut butter is what guaranteed our adult acceptance of this exotic Asian dip. The peanut sauce keeps very well, and nothing tastes better than a spicy smidge on grilled chicken, pork, or shrimp kebabs or satay. Cold rice noodles dressed with peanut sauce are pretty special, too.

4 garlic cloves, crushed

3 tablespoons chopped cilantro leaves or 1 tablespoon minced roots

2 fresh red chilies, seeded and chopped

¼ cup dark soy sauce

2 tablespoons Asian fish sauce (*nam pla* or *nuoc mam*)

1 tablespoon fresh lime juice

1 cup smooth peanut butter

1 tablespoon toasted sesame oil

½ cup unsweetened coconut milk

¼ cup unsalted roasted peanuts, chopped

Mince the garlic, cilantro, and chilies in a food processor. Add the soy, fish sauce, and lime juice and puree. Blend in the peanut butter and oil and add the coconut milk in two parts so you can adjust the consistency. Fold in the peanuts.

COOK'S NOTES: *You can warm the refrigerated sauce in the microwave to bring it to room temperature for dipping.*

You can substitute mint or basil for the cilantro.

QUICK HORS D'OEUVRE:

Mix ½ cup peanut sauce, ¼ cup minced scallions (with some of the green part), and 1 tablespoon mayonnaise. Spread on sesame rice crackers and put under the broiler for a minute until they puff. Sprinkle with crispy bacon bits or additional herbs.

A QUICK PEANUT SAUCE:

Combine ¼ cup peanut butter with 2 tablespoons hoisin sauce, 1 teaspoon chili paste with garlic or Thai chili sauce, 1 tablespoon fish sauce or dark soy, and 1 tablespoon ketchup. Thin with ¼ cup coconut milk, chicken broth, or water.

SESAME DIPPING SAUCE

Makes about ¾ cup

These savory Pacific Rim flavors will enliven raw vegetables, seafood, and skewered meats. The sauce also makes a splendid dressing for The Poached Chicken cold (page 51). If you like hummus, you'll be glad to find another use for that jar of tahini in back of the fridge.

2½ tablespoons sesame paste

2 tablespoons Asian chili sauce

2 tablespoons safflower or canola oil

2 teaspoons sesame oil

1½ tablespoons soy sauce

1½ teaspoons balsamic vinegar

2 tablespoons chicken broth

Whisk all the ingredients to combine. Store in screw-top jar in the refrigerator. Keeps for weeks.

COOK'S NOTES: *Chinese black vinegar is the authentic choice, but it isn't widely available. Substituting balsamic vinegar adds a pleasant hint of sweetness to this spicy dip.*

ZESTY ORANGE DIPPING SAUCE

Makes about ½ cup

This is one of those spontaneous inventions worth recording. It's a simple keeper recipe, great for dipping chicken, pork, or spareribs and it's also a divine glaze for stir-fried shrimp or scallops. (See instructions in Cook's Notes below.)

2 tablespoons frozen orange juice
 concentrate, thawed
1 teaspoon grated gingerroot
2 tablespoons maple syrup
1 teaspoon Thai or Vietnamese sriracha
 sauce (available in Asian or specialty
 food stores) or another hot chili
 sauce

2 tablespoons soy sauce
1 tablespoon sherry vinegar or rice
 wine vinegar

Whisk together all the ingredients in a microwave-safe bowl. Heat on high for 30 seconds to 1 minute, whisk again, and allow the sauce to cool. Store in a screw-top jar. It will keep indefinitely.

COOK'S NOTES: *To use this sauce as a shrimp or scallop glaze, stir-fry the seafood in a little oil and garlic, while reducing the sauce in a separate pan until it thickens a little and becomes somewhat syrupy. Pour the sauce over the seafood and stir to glaze.*

FIVE-SPICE BABY CARROTS

Makes about 1½ cups

There's more than one way to get your vegetables and more than one way to enjoy those irresistible baby carrots.

½ pound baby carrots, preferably organic

1 teaspoon Chinese five-spice powder

Pinch of cayenne pepper (optional)

¼ teaspoon kosher salt

1 quarter-size slice of ginger, unpeeled

1 garlic clove, cut in half

1 cup water

1½ tablespoons honey

1 tablespoon lime juice

Select carrots of somewhat equal size, ignoring the very thin and the very thick. Place them in a medium sauté pan with a lid with all the ingredients except the honey and lime juice. Bring the water to a simmer, cover the pan, and cook for about 10 minutes or until the carrots are almost tender. Add the honey and lime juice and raise the heat to high. The liquid will evaporate and form a glaze, but check the carrots; if they begin to soften before the glaze forms, remove them with a slotted spoon. Continue the reduction and as soon as it becomes thick and syrupy; pour it over the carrots and toss to coat. Cool to serve or store.

RED ONION CONFIT

Makes about 1½ cups

Here's a quickly prepared little condiment that lends an unusual flavor fillip to lamb, chicken, veal, or swordfish. I like it a lot on cold turkey sandwiches.

¼ cup olive oil

2 cups chopped red onion

Kosher salt

1 tablespoon hot chili sauce, or to taste

1 teaspoon grated orange zest

¼ cup currants plumped in hot orange juice

Heat the oil and sauté the onion for about 5 minutes over medium heat to soften. Turn up the heat and sauté until golden. Salt to taste.

Stir in the chili sauce and orange zest and combine. Drain the currants and fold them in. Cool and store in screw-top jars. The confit will keep for several weeks refrigerated.

REFRIGERATOR PICKLES

Makes about 10 pickles

My love of pickles goes back to the neighborhood Jewish deli of my childhood. It never occurred to me that I could make my own, and I can't—at least not those wonderful barrel pickles of my youth. One of my more talented restaurant chefs used to turn out the best luncheon pickles overnight, so as long as I had him and his pickles I didn't even try. Then came Chris Schlesinger and John Willoughby's book *Quick Pickles!* and I was back in pickle heaven. Using their simple procedure and my seasonings, here's one of my successful batches. If you don't see pickling cucumbers in your supermarket, try a specialty food store. Any good Asian market also stocks them. I have no luck with English cucumbers; although some say they work, they refuse to crisp for me.

1½ pounds Kirby or pickling cucumbers
1 small red onion, cut in quarters
5 tablespoons kosher salt
Fresh sprigs of dill
1½ cups cider vinegar

1½ cups water
2 tablespoons pickling spice
1 dried hot chili, stemmed, split, with seeds
6 garlic cloves, split

❧ Remove a thin slice from the stem end of the cucumbers and discard. Slice them thickly crosswise, or lengthwise into fat wedges. Cut one onion wedge crosswise into 1-inch sections and separate the layers. Place the cucumbers and onion in a stainless steel or ceramic bowl and sprinkle in 3 tablespoons of the salt. Toss well and cover with ice cubes. Refrigerate the bowl for 1 to 2 hours. Drain and rinse twice to remove the salt. Pack the cucumbers and onion alternately in widemouthed jars or lidded crocks. Tuck the dill sprigs around the edge and down the middle.

Combine the remaining ingredients in a saucepan and bring the mixture to a boil to dissolve the salt. Pour the brine over the pickles to cover and allow them to cool at room temperature. Seal and refrigerate. They can be eaten the next day, but flavor develops best in a couple of days.

COOK'S NOTES: *Keeping the proportion of vegetables to brine the same, you can add other vegetables for color contrast. Carrot slices, red and/or green pepper squares, and thin zucchini slices work well. You can also substitute seasonings of your choice such as fennel seeds, mustard seeds, cumin or celery seeds, peppercorns, turmeric, or bay leaves.*
Kept refrigerated, these pickles should keep for a week or two.

ASIAN PEAR and MANGO CHUTNEY

Makes about 1½ quarts

Homemade fresh fruit chutneys are really fun to prepare and make such an exuberant statement that they can outclass simple roasts or grilled meat. Further, it's a practical way to rescue the orphans of the family fruit bowl. Once you make it, you will realize how easy it is to balance the sweet, sour, and spicy essence of a good chutney. You need only to remember to save the fruit from overcooking while reducing the glaze. Simply remove the fruit, continue the sauce reduction, and then pour the sauce over the fruit. The chutney will set up perfectly when it cools. Almost any firm fruits, in compatible combinations, will make superlative chutney.

3 Asian pears, peeled and chopped

3 large semi-ripe mangoes, peeled and diced

¼ cup finely chopped crystallized ginger

¼ cup dried currants

2 garlic cloves, crushed and minced

1 tablespoon mustard seeds

1 tablespoon minced hot green chilies

½ cup rice wine vinegar

¼ cup balsamic vinegar

½ cup dark brown sugar

1 teaspoon kosher salt

Place all the ingredients in a shallow microwave-safe dish covered with plastic wrap and cook in the microwave on high for 5 minutes. Stir and taste. Adjust the tart/sweet balance if necessary and continue cooking uncovered, in 5-minute intervals once or twice, checking the fruit after each interval. If the fruit softens before the juices become syrupy, remove it with a slotted spoon and continue reducing the sauce. Pour the thickened sauce over the fruit. Store the chutney in clean, widemouthed screw-top jars, allowing it to cool completely before sealing and storing in the refrigerator. It will keep several weeks.

PRUNE PLUM and BLACK MISSION FIG CHUTNEY

Makes about 1½ quarts

This is an early fall chutney, perfect for when the prune plums and figs are in the market and you're looking for an excuse to buy them. I'm still working on a big batch I made last year and recently wowed friends by serving the chutney on top of a mediocre over-ripe Brie, along with drinks. I've even smeared it on a cream cheese sandwich with walnut bread.

1½ pounds prune plums, pitted and cut in eighths

½ pound black mission figs, chopped

¼ cup raisins

4 large shallots, thinly sliced

4 garlic cloves, finely chopped

1 to 2 hot red chilies, stemmed, seeded, and minced

4 quarter-size slices of ginger, julienned

1 teaspoon kosher salt

½ cup rice wine vinegar

½ cup unsweetened coconut milk

Place all the ingredients in a large, shallow microwave-safe dish, cover with plastic wrap, and cook on high for 5 minutes. Uncover, taste for seasoning, and cook for another 5 minutes checking after 3 minutes or until the fruit is tender. The figs should make this chutney sweet enough, but you can always add some sugar or honey to taste.

COOK'S NOTES: *Even if you aren't entirely satisfied with the seasoning after the chutney cools, you can reheat and adjust. All fruit differs in ripeness and sweetness, and adjustments are inevitable. For a spicier chutney, stir in some cayenne or hot sauce. For a more tart chutney, drizzle in additional vinegar or fresh lemon or lime juice.*

HOLIDAY CRANBERRY CHUTNEY

Makes 2 quarts

T*his chutney is a wonderful change* from the traditional cranberry sauce served at Thanksgiving and complements the rich meat of roast turkey extremely well. It has won raves from my most conservative holiday guests. The chutney keeps for weeks in the refrigerator and makes a welcome Christmas gift.

1 pound cranberries, washed and picked over	Grated zest of 2 oranges
1/2 cup granulated sugar	1/4 cup frozen orange juice concentrate
2 Asian pears, peeled and cubed	1/4 cup rice wine vinegar
2 Bosc or Comice pears, peeled, cored, and cubed	1/4 cup balsamic vinegar
1 Granny Smith apple, peeled, and cubed	Sugar, preferably superfine
	1 teaspoon kosher salt
1/4 cup ginger preserves	12 canned water chestnuts, rinsed and thickly sliced
1 to 2 jalapeño peppers, stemmed, seeded, and slivered	3/4 cup walnut pieces or chopped pecans, toasted

Place the washed cranberries in a covered microwave-safe dish with the granulated sugar and cook on high 3 to 4 minutes until the berries pop. Remove the berries with a slotted spoon and reserve.

Add the pears, apple, ginger preserves, peppers, orange zest, and concentrate to the remaining juice. Stir to combine; add the vinegars, a light sprinkling of sugar, and the salt. Taste the juice and make your first seasoning adjustments, if needed. Cover with plastic wrap, return it to the microwave, and cook on high for 5 minutes. If the fruit is soft, remove it with a slotted spoon and add it to the cranberries. If it's not yet ready, return the mixture to the oven, uncovered, and continue cooking and checking the fruit at 3-minute intervals.

With the fruit removed, continue cooking all of the juices, including those from the fruit you set aside, until they reduce to a syrupy glaze. When you've achieved the desired consistency, taste again for any last-minute seasoning adjustments. Return the fruit to the glaze and stir to combine.

Allow the chutney to cool to room temperature before stirring in the water chestnuts and nuts. Pack in clean screw-top jars and refrigerate. It will keep for weeks.

TOMATILLO and GREEN CHILI SALSA

Makes 3 cups

Have you often wondered what you should do with those curious giant green berries that look like a mini-tomato in a hula skirt? Even if you've eaten tomatillos in Mexican restaurants or seen them listed as ingredients in recipes, they do look a bit daunting in the produce section. Take some home; they make a terrific salsa that works as a dip, an accent ingredient, or a sauce.

1 pound tomatillos	1/2 medium onion, chopped
1 large jalapeño pepper	1 teaspoon kosher salt
2 Anaheim peppers or 1 poblano	1/2 cup lime juice
1 serrano pepper	1 1/2 teaspoons sugar
2 garlic cloves, chopped	1/3 cup chopped cilantro

Peel the husks from the tomatillos and rinse off the sticky sap underneath. Roast them along with the peppers on a large dry griddle, or over an open flame, until their skins blister and blacken. Place the peppers in a plastic bag for a few minutes to loosen the skins.

Rub off the charred skin, pull off the stems, and remove the seeds and veins. Combine all of the ingredients in a food processor or blender along with any reserved tomatillo liquid and pulse to combine, leaving the sauce well mixed but somewhat chunky. Taste for seasoning. It should be pleasantly tart but not astringent. You may need a tad more sugar for balance. Pack in screw-top jars and refrigerate. It will keep for weeks.

COOK'S NOTES: *Use the salsa for dipping, or add some to a mashed avocado for a delightful variation on guacamole. Puree the salsa with some vegetable or chicken broth and a bit of cream for a delicious sauce for chicken, pork, or fish.*

DRY FRIED CORN and AVOCADO SALSA

Although this is a good salsa to prepare when corn is in season, it works almost as well with frozen kernels. You can make the base and add the avocado, lime juice, and cilantro when you're ready to serve.

2 cups young corn kernels, fresh or
    frozen and thawed
1/3 cup finely chopped red onion
1/3 cup diced red bell pepper
1/2 cup canned black turtle beans, rinsed
1/4 cup safflower oil

1 teaspoon chili powder
1 avocado, pitted and diced
6 young radishes, slivered (optional)
1 1/2 tablespoons lime juice
1/3 cup chopped cilantro
Salt and freshly ground black pepper

 If you're using thawed frozen corn, blot it dry on paper towels. Heat a skillet and add the corn. Fry over medium-high heat, tossing often, until the kernels start to pop and pick up flecks of brown. (They will smell toasted when they're ready.) Set aside to cool.

Combine the corn with the onion, red pepper, and black beans. Pour the oil in a small microwave-safe dish, add the chili powder, and heat in the microwave on high for 20 to 30 seconds. When the oil is cool, pour it over the combined mixture. Either store the base of the salsa for several days in the refrigerator, adding the rest of the ingredients when you're ready to serve, or toss it all together, season to taste, and serve immediately.

TROPICAL FRUIT SALSA

Makes about 1 quart

*M*angoes and papayas are plentiful and ripen quickly at home, and fresh pineapple is finally coming to market both ripe and extra sweet. There is nothing more refreshing than a chilled mélange of these tropical beauties to accompany a grilled or roast chicken or barbecued pork ribs. I also like it with grilled jumbo shrimp or any firm-fleshed white fish such as swordfish, halibut, or snapper. All you need is a bowl of lightly buttered, aromatic jasmine rice to complete the meal.

2 cups diced mangoes
1 cup diced papaya, half the seeds reserved and well rinsed
1 cup diced fresh pineapple
6 to 8 scallions, slivered with some of the green
¼ cup julienned mint leaves
¼ cup safflower oil

1 teaspoon grated gingerroot
1 red jalapeño pepper, seeded and minced
2 tablespoons lime juice
Kosher salt and white pepper
Pinch of superfine sugar
¼ cup plain yogurt

Combine the mangoes, papaya, pineapple, scallions, and mint. Combine all the rest of the ingredients, including the reserved papaya seeds, in a screw-top jar and shake vigorously. Sample the dressing and adjust to taste. Either store the fruit and dressing separately for a couple of days, or combine and serve. Be sure to chill the salsa thoroughly before serving.

CREAMY GARLIC SAUCE

Makes about 2 cups

This surprisingly subtle sauce keeps for a long time in the fridge, successfully freezes, reheats well, and has multiple personalities. You can infuse the broth with saffron, or squeeze in a little sun-dried tomato or anchovy paste. You can add chipotle puree, fresh herbs and lemon zest, or roasted red pepper puree. You can even thin it out with more broth for a lovely garlic soup with croutons. It's one of those flavor-enhancing basics you'll be very happy to have on hand.

1½ cups Chicken Broth (page 4), preferably homemade

4 shallots, chopped

2 heads garlic, peeled and left whole

Kosher salt and white pepper

Pinch of cayenne pepper

¼ cup crème fraîche

 Place the broth, shallots, and garlic in a saucepan and bring to a boil. Reduce the heat, cover the pan, and simmer for about 20 minutes or until the garlic is very tender. Allow the mixture to cool slightly before adding it to the blender with the remaining ingredients. Puree until smooth and taste for seasoning. Store in a screw-top jar.

TOMATO CONCASSÉ

Makes about 2 cups

*H*ere's another quick basic with great versatility. This recipe should come to mind when your kitchen counter is full of dead-ripe homegrown tomatoes and you can't face another BLT. I can't think of anything, with the exception of duck, that this sauce wouldn't enhance. Stir in a little of the Creamy Garlic Sauce (page 141), and serve as a sauce for a sautéed beef fillet steak.

6 to 8 tomatoes, peeled, cored, and
 halved
2 tablespoons olive oil
½ cup chopped sweet onion

1 garlic clove, smashed and minced
Kosher salt and freshly ground
 black pepper
¾ cup dry red wine

Squeeze the tomato halves lightly to remove the seeds and use your fingertips to push out the rest. Roughly chop the tomatoes and set aside.

Heat the oil and add the onion and garlic. Cook them over medium-high heat and add the tomatoes, salt, and pepper. Cook the mixture briefly to distribute the flavors but do not let the tomatoes lose their texture. Drain the solids from the pan with a slotted spoon, leaving as much liquid as possible in the pan. Add the wine and reduce the liquid by half. Turn off the heat, add back the tomato mixture, and allow it to cool in the pan. Store in screw-top jars in the refrigerator, where it will keep 2 to 3 weeks, or freeze if you have to keep it longer.

LEMON-CHIVE SAUCE

Makes 1 cup

T*he pleasant tang and pucker of a light lemon sauce* is just what a fish fillet or shellfish needs to bring it to life, not to mention the otherwise pallid chicken breast or odd steamed vegetable. Below are several variations that may spark other ideas. This sauce will keep a week or more in the refrigerator, but since it's so quick and simple to make, I suggest doubling the recipe and keeping some in the freezer.

1 tablespoon butter	1 tablespoon lemon juice
1½ tablespoons flour	¾ cup vegetable, chicken, or fish broth
Kosher salt and white pepper	½ teaspoon grated lemon zest
Pinch of cayenne	1 tablespoon snipped chives

Melt the butter in a small saucepan and whisk in the flour. Cook over low heat for 1 minute and add the salt, pepper, and cayenne. Pour in the liquids a little bit at a time, whisking constantly to smooth out any lumps. Stir in the lemon zest and chives. Store in the refrigerator or freezer.

VARIATIONS:

Add ¼ cup heavy cream and simmer to reduce and thicken.

Add minced dill, sage, parsley, mint, or basil in combination with the chives.

Omit the salt, substitute clam broth, and add ¼ cup heavy cream. Add cooked seafood of your choice and serve over pasta, without cheese.

Omit the flour. Increase the amount of broth to 1 cup. Beat two egg yolks until thick, whisk in a little hot broth to temper, and whisk the eggs into the sauce. Cook over very low heat, whisking constantly, until the sauce thickens.

CHINESE LEMON SAUCE

Makes 1 cup

½ cup fresh lemon juice, strained
2 tablespoons sugar
¼ cup Chicken Broth (page 4)
2 tablespoons soy sauce
Pinch of kosher salt

2 quarter-size slices of ginger, unpeeled
   and lightly crushed
Grated zest of 1 lemon
1 tablespoon cornstarch mixed with
   1 tablespoon water

Bring all the ingredients to a boil except the cornstarch slurry. Reduce the heat and simmer for 1 minute to release the flavor of the ginger. Remove the ginger and discard. Stir in the slurry and whisk until thickened. Taste for seasoning. Add more salt or sugar if needed.

SALSA de CHILI COLORADO

Red Chili Sauce

This is the sauce I use to make chili con carne and keep on hand for spontaneous tacos and enchiladas. I've also used it to lightly sauce boneless smoked pork chops and thick slices of cooked turkey breast—a great supper with black beans and rice. With the addition of 3 tablespoons of cider vinegar and a little more sugar, it makes a wonderful marinade for grilled or roast chicken and meat. Dried chilies are now readily available. Look for them in the produce section of specialty food stores and displayed on carousels in some supermarkets.

4 large dried Ancho chilies, or half New
    Mexico or Guajillo
2 tablespoons safflower or canola oil
1½ cups chicken broth or water, heated
3 garlic cloves, smashed and minced

¾ teaspoon ground cumin
¾ teaspoon dried oregano, preferably
    Mexican
½ teaspoon kosher salt
½ teaspoon sugar

Pull the stems from the chilies and shake out the seeds. Slit the chili in half and open it out flat—it doesn't matter if it's in pieces.

Heat the oil and toast the chili pieces for a few seconds on each side, watching closely so they don't scorch. Remove them to a small bowl and cover them with the hot broth. Allow them to rehydrate for about 30 minutes.

Place all the ingredients, including the soaking liquid, into the food processor or blender and puree until smooth. Taste, and adjust the seasoning if necessary. The small amount of sugar should have softened the slightly bitter edge of the chilies. Allow the sauce to cool before refrigerating or freezing.

FRESH TOMATO SAUCE with SAFFRON and RAISINS

Serves 4

I think firm, meaty fish needs a sauce. This one has the kind of *agrodolce* character that complements any hearty fish fillet. I think it would also be terrific on fettucine.

3 tablespoons olive oil
½ cup chopped red onion
Pinch of saffron threads
6 ripe summer tomatoes, peeled,
    seeded, and chopped

Kosher salt and freshly ground
    black pepper
Pinch of sugar
2 tablespoons raisins
2 tablespoons sherry vinegar

Heat the oil in a deep sauté pan and cook the onion until it softens and turns translucent. Crumble the saffron over the onion and stir to combine. Add the tomatoes, salt, pepper, sugar, and raisins. Cook over medium-low heat until the tomatoes soften and the watery liquid evaporates.

Add the vinegar 1 tablespoon at a time, tasting as you go. Add more salt and sugar if necessary.

Allow the sauce to cool before storing in the refrigerator, where it will keep for several days. It does not freeze well.

TOMATOES: PEELED, SEEDED, AND PULPED

Peel tomatoes by dropping them into boiling water for a few seconds until the skin begins to pucker. If you have only one or two, spear the stem with a fork and either hold it in boiling water or rotate it over a gas flame. The first little split in the skin signals it's ready. Hold the impaled tomato in one hand and peel it with a paring knife with the other hand.

To seed a tomato, cut it in half and squeeze gently over the sink to release the seeds. Push out whatever remains with the tip of your finger.

To pulp a tomato, seed it first and then cut out the interior flesh with a paring knife, leaving the shell to dice or julienne.

BARBECUE SAUCE

Makes 2 cups

Why are there so many recipes for barbecue sauce, and is there room for one more? The answer to the first part lies in the number of times you've doctored a bottled sauce or even a homemade one, trying to get it right. Is there room for another recipe? You bet, and here's mine.

1/4 cup safflower or canola oil	1 tablespoon Worcestershire sauce
1 medium onion, chopped	2 tablespoons cider vinegar
4 garlic cloves, chopped	2 tablespoons lime juice
1 tablespoon chopped fresh gingerroot, or 1 teaspoon powdered	1/3 cup strong coffee
2 tablespoons chili powder	1/2 cup maple syrup
1 teaspoon kosher salt	3/4 cup ketchup
1 tablespoon chopped bottled jalapeño peppers	

 Place the oil, onion, garlic, ginger, chili powder, salt, and jalapeños in a food processor and puree. Scrape the mixture into a saucepan and add the remaining ingredients. Bring the sauce to a simmer and cook for 5 minutes.

Taste and adjust the seasoning, if needed. (Remember that the meat will not taste as spicy as the sauce alone.) Cool the sauce before storing. It can be frozen.

MANGO CHUTNEY BARBECUE SAUCE

Makes 1 cup

The familiar Anglo-Indian bottled chutney is made with dried fruit, in this case mango, and its inherent flavor intensity tends to limit its use. This recipe gives you a good reason for emptying that jar in the back of your fridge. It's a particularly complementary sauce for lamb, duck, chicken, or spareribs.

You can be generous in basting with this sauce, since it's not as acidic or assertive as a tomato-based one. I like to pass around a separate bowl of it at the table.

2 tablespoons safflower or canola oil

1 teaspoon chili oil

5 tablespoons Major Grey's mango chutney

2 garlic cloves, chopped

1 large shallot, chopped

1/4 teaspoon kosher salt

3 tablespoons soy sauce

1 1/2 tablespoons lime juice

2 teaspoons sherry vinegar

2 to 3 tablespoons honey

1/3 cup minced cilantro

 Place the oils, chutney, garlic, shallot, and salt in a food processor and puree. Scrape the mixture into a skillet and simmer it for 2 to 3 minutes.

Whisk in the soy sauce, lime juice, and vinegar. Add the honey, 1 tablespoon at a time, tasting as you go and adjusting the sweet/tart balance to your taste. Fold in the cilantro.

Allow the sauce to cool before storing in a screw-top jar. It will keep in the fridge for weeks.

LEEK and FENNEL PASTA SAUCE

Serves 4 to 6

The combination of leeks and fennel with a hint of garlic is irresistible and even more so on spaghetti with a sprinkle of Parmigiano-Reggiano. If you have any left over, it's delectable layered with thinly sliced Yukon Gold potatoes in a creamy gratin.

3 tablespoons butter

2 tablespoons olive oil

3 leeks, green part trimmed, thoroughly washed and thinly sliced

1 fennel bulb, stalks removed, green fronds reserved

2 garlic cloves, sliced and slivered

1/4 teaspoon red pepper flakes

Kosher salt and freshly ground black pepper

1 1/2 cups Vegetable Broth (page 8) or Chicken Broth (page 4), preferably homemade

2 medium ripe tomatoes, peeled, pulped, and finely diced

 Heat the butter and oil in a large sauté pan and add the sliced leeks. Cut off the base of the fennel and the tough outer shell. Stand the bulb on its base and slice the fennel. Add the slices to the leeks along with the garlic, red pepper flakes, salt, and pepper. Toss to combine.

Add the broth, bring to a simmer, and cover the pan. Cook for 20 to 30 minutes or until the vegetables are very soft. Scrape them into a food processor and puree them.

Mince the fennel fronds for garnish.

Either fold the diced tomato shells into the sauce or save them separately for garnish along with the fennel fronds.

This sauce will keep in a screw-top jar in the refrigerator for several days, or it can be frozen.

BOLOGNESE MEAT SAUCE

Makes 2½ cups

A classic *ragù alla Bolognese* should only be homemade, and it's very simple to make. It can be used as is to sauce tagliatelle, to layer lasagne, or to fill cannelloni. It keeps several days in the refrigerator and freezes well.

2 tablespoons butter

1 tablespoon extra-virgin olive oil

¼ pound lean pancetta, minced

½ medium red onion, diced

1 medium carrot, diced

2 inner celery stalks, diced

¾ pound beef chuck, ground once

½ pound pork, ground once

3 tablespoons tomato paste

Pinch of cloves

A couple of gratings of nutmeg

Kosher salt and freshly ground black pepper

½ cup white wine

1 cup Beef Broth (page 6)

½ cup heavy cream

Heat the butter and oil in a deep sauté pan or Dutch oven and lightly brown the pancetta. Add the onion, carrot, and celery and continue cooking until the vegetables are soft. Add the meat and sauté it until no redness remains.

Add the tomato paste, cloves, nutmeg, salt, pepper, and wine. Add ¼ cup of the beef broth. Bring the mixture to a simmer. Cover the pan and reduce the heat to low, using a heat diffuser over a gas flame. Slowly simmer the sauce for about 1½ to 2 hours, adding the rest of the broth in ¼-cup increments. Remove the lid after an hour. The finished sauce should be very thick. Add the cream and simmer for another 10 minutes.

OKRA and ROASTED TOMATO SAUCE

Serves 4

Fresh okra used to be found only in farmers' markets, but now it's increasingly stocked in supermarkets. Always look for blemish-free okra, about 2 inches in length and heavy for its size. There should be no fear of stickiness with this tasty recipe. Whatever liquid this petite vegetable exudes is a natural sauce thickener.

You could also sauté the okra whole over high heat, which is another way to prevent stickiness, and serve this as a side dish.

3 tablespoons extra-virgin olive oil
1/4 cup chopped onion
3 garlic cloves, smashed and minced
1/4 teaspoon red pepper flakes
1 pound small fresh okra, thickly sliced
1/4 pound smoked ham, slivered
  (optional)

One 14 1/2-ounce can plum tomatoes,
  preferably Muir Glen's Fire-Roasted
Kosher salt and freshly ground
  black pepper

 Heat the olive oil and sauté the onion, garlic, and pepper flakes until the onion is soft. Remove the mixture from the pan and set aside.

Add the okra and ham to the hot oil and stir-fry quickly until the edges of the okra start to brown. Return the onion mixture to the pan along with the tomatoes. Simmer over low heat until the sauce thickens. Season with salt and pepper.

The sauce will keep several days in the refrigerator but will suffer a bit if frozen.

COOK'S NOTES: *Choose a sturdy enough pasta to stand up to this sauce. A tubular-shape like penne regate would be the perfect choice. You could also toss the cooked pasta and sauce together with diced Fontina cheese, sprinkle it with Parmigiano-Reggiano, and bake it in a gratin dish in a 350° oven until the cheese melts.*

WALNUT SAUCE for PASTA

Serves 4

This is a wonderful sauce over cheese ravioli or tossed with linguine or tagliatelle. I served it once as a first course at a dinner party and substituted unsalted pistachios for the walnuts and minced parsley for the marjoram. It looked, and tasted, amazing.

- 2 tablespoons butter
- 1 tablespoon olive oil
- 2 garlic cloves, cut in half
- 1/2 cup chopped walnuts
- Kosher salt and freshly ground black pepper

- 1/4 teaspoon dried marjoram
- 1 day-old slice of good bakery bread, preferably Italian
- 1 cup light cream, or half and half
- 1/3 cup grated Parmigiano-Reggiano

 Heat the butter and oil in a small skillet and cook the garlic over low heat until it's soft. Remove garlic and discard. Add the walnuts and toast them lightly. (Be careful not to scorch them.) Season with salt, pepper, and marjoram.

Crumble the bread in a small bowl and add enough cream to barely cover it.

Set aside a few of the nuts for garnish and place the remaining nuts in a food processor or blender. Squeeze out the bread, saving the cream in a separate bowl, and add the bread to the food processor along with the cheese. Puree the mixture to a paste and then slowly add in the cream until you have a fairly thick sauce.

The finished sauce will keep for several days in the refrigerator, or you can freeze the base and add the cream when you're ready to use it.

PASTA SAUCE MONDELLO

Serves 4

I *learned how to make this midnight pasta sauce* from a dashing Siciliano in Palermo many years ago. It's every bit as seductive now as it was then—well, almost.

3 tablespoons unsalted butter

2 garlic cloves, smashed and minced

4 shallots, minced

1 cup stemmed and chopped porcini or cremini mushrooms

3 paper-thin slices prosciutto di Parma, fat removed and slivered

12 fresh sage leaves, stacked and slivered

3 plum tomatoes, peeled, pulped, and slivered

2 tablespoons tomato paste

3/4 cup light cream or half and half

Kosher salt and freshly ground black pepper

Freshly grated nutmeg

Freshly grated Parmigiano-Reggiano

Heat the butter in a large sauté pan and toss the garlic, shallots, and mushrooms over medium-high heat to soften the shallots and brown the mushrooms. If the mushrooms exude dark juice, pour it off so the final sauce won't turn an unattractive gray. Add additional butter to compensate for the loss of some of the juices.

Add the prosciutto and sage and sauté until the ham is slightly frizzled. Add the tomatoes, tomato paste, and cream. Reduce the sauce over medium-high heat briefly, about 2 to 3 minutes. The sauce should be rather thin and a pretty pale pink. Season with salt and pepper to taste.

Garnish the sauced pasta with the nutmeg and Parmigiano-Reggiano immediately before serving.

The sauce will keep in the refrigerator for 3 to 4 days. Freezing is not recommended.

FRESH RED and YELLOW TOMATO SAUCE with BASIL and CAPERS

Serves 4

Nothing new in this recipe, but it's one of summer's most delightful and refreshing suppers, and I tend to forget about it. Only dead-ripe farm stand tomatoes will do.

- 2 ripe tomatoes, seeded and chopped
- 2 ripe yellow tomatoes, seeded and chopped
- 4 garlic cloves, smashed and minced
- 1/4 cup finely chopped red onion
- 3 tablespoons minced flat-leaf parsley
- 2 tablespoons fat capers, chopped
- 2 tablespoons Kalamata olives, pitted and slivered (optional)
- Kosher salt and lots of freshly ground black pepper
- 1/4 cup extra-virgin olive oil
- 2 tablespoons red wine vinegar or lemon juice

 Toss all the ingredients together in a bowl and taste for seasoning. Chill well before serving over the piping hot pasta of your choice tossed with Parmigiano-Reggiano.

You can keep the mixture, tightly covered, in the refrigerator for 3 to 4 days without salt and vinegar. Before using, drain off any water from the tomatoes and add the salt and the vinegar.

ROASTED GARLIC

Garlic is a wondrous thing and so useful in so many different ways. Roasting or poaching it transforms the cloves' flavor from assertive to tender and mild. The fresher the garlic the better; don't use bulbs with green sprouts or dried-out bulbs with their paper husks falling off. The garlic capital of the United States—Gilroy, California—sends out its fresh crop in the summer, and often you can find their braided chains of garlic in most stores, which always encourages me to roast away and tuck the paste in the freezer for winter. Pink garlic comes from Mexico in the spring and has a splendid mild flavor.

To Roast: Preheat the oven to 325° (the toaster oven is fine). Remove the loose outer layers of husk. Cut off the top third of the bulb to expose the tips of the cloves. Stand three bulbs on a length of foil, drizzle them with olive oil, and season with salt and pepper. Crease and fold the foil over the top and twist the ends tightly. Roast for 1 hour. When the garlic has cooled, squeeze the soft, fragrant flesh from the cloves like toothpaste from a tube. Mix it with a little olive oil to make a velvety paste. It freezes well. I often mix it with a small amount of mayonnaise and keep it in the refrigerator to add to dressings, sauces, or soups.

Here's a real bonus for roasting garlic: Place any number of trimmed bulbs in a small baking dish and submerge the garlic two thirds of the way up with olive oil. Cover the top with fresh herbs of your choice, such as rosemary, thyme, sage, or tarragon. Seal the dish with foil and bake at 325° for 1½ hours. Funnel the seasoned oil into a bottle and use it for salad dressings, homemade Blender Mayonnaise (page 120), or sautéing. Make a paste of the garlic with a little of the seasoned oil and smear it on top of a steak or lamb chop or under the skin of a roasting chicken.

Red Wine and Roasted Garlic Sauce: Reduce ½ cup red wine and ½ cup Beef Broth (page 6) by half, or until it is syrupy—about 10 minutes. Whisk in 3 tablespoons softened herb butter (see Compound Butters, page 118) mixed with 1 tablespoon Roasted Garlic. Add salt and pepper. This is a delicious quick sauce for beef or lamb.

SWEETS AND TREATS

6

I f this book has hit its mark, you are about to spend a wildly productive, hum-a-happy-tune day in your kitchen. The soup stock will simmer, the midweek pork will curry, and back-up meatballs will roll into the freezer with a jar of roasted garlic, while the cucumbers pickle. You will make a sauce for tonight's pasta or a salsa for the chicken waiting to be grilled. You will, of course, feel both virtuous and content. Cooking hasn't been this much fun in a long time.

So where's the treat? Family or friends who wander into your domain at the end of the day, inevitably led by their noses to an aromatic kitchen, will beg for instant gratification. Leave some time to make cookies, a basket of breakfast muffins, a keeping cake, some savory nuts to snack on before dinner, or the ultimate treat—a box of chocolate truffles.

If there's no ice cream in the freezer, there must be fruit or juice you can freeze into granita. Not the same mouth-feel, of course, but it's mighty refreshing.

The trusty microwave makes wonderful quick homemade jam from seasonal fruit. And now that you've set aside a little free time for your favorite hobby, be sure to candy some of that citrus peel that will otherwise end up in the disposal.

I've included some things in this chapter—which easily could have been the lengthiest in the book—that are perfect stowaways for company, expected or not.

Most of all, these recipes should remind you of personal favorite treats you've forgotten that might also be perfect keepers. It's all about planning ahead.

CANDIED CITRUS PEEL

Makes about 1½ cups

*W*hat a pity to toss away all those delicious orange, tangerine, lemon, and grapefruit peels when they're so perfectly delicious candied. Candied peel is so easy to make, and sometimes a few sweet bites can be just the right finish to a meal. They can be minced and sprinkled over sherbet or ice cream, used to decorate cakes or pudding, or presented with Chocolate Truffles (page 180) for a superb dessert for company. Packed in a decorative jar, candied peel will be a more welcome hostess gift than the ubiquitous bottle of wine.

3 large navel oranges or 4 large lemons or 4 tangerines or 2 large grapefruit (or a combination of citrus)	1 cup water 1 cup granulated sugar Superfine sugar for coating

Use a vegetable peeler to cut wide, thin slices of rind from the fruit, removing as little of the white pith as possible. Trim the ragged edges from the rind, wasting as little as you can, to make the edges straight. Cut each piece into julienned strips about ⅛ inch wide. Place the peel in a saucepan and cover with water. Bring to a boil and drain. Repeat the process twice. The third time, bring the peel to a boil, simmer for 10 minutes, and drain thoroughly.

Combine 1 cup water and the granulated sugar and bring to a boil. Add the peel and cook over low heat until the syrup falls from a spoon in a thin thread.

Sprinkle a layer of superfine sugar on a cookie sheet, remove the peels from the syrup with tongs, and lay them on the sugar. Toss them around to coat and leave them to dry overnight. Pack into screw-top jars and refrigerate. They'll keep for months.

COOK'S NOTES: *You can also candy slivers of peeled fresh gingerroot in the same manner. Increase the simmering time after the second blanching to 30 minutes.*

To preserve soft ginger in syrup, proceed as above but add a couple of tablespoons of corn syrup to the sugar-water. Drop in the ginger, simmer over low heat until the syrup thickens to the soft ball stage (230°), and take it off the heat to steep. When it has cooled, store it in screw-top jars in the refrigerator.

FIG and PEAR JAM

Makes about 3 cups

When fresh fruit is plentiful, you can forget buying those expensive jams or preserves. The microwave does a marvelous job making chunky jam for your morning toast, and it goes so quickly that you'll wonder why you haven't thought of it before. Fresh figs have a short season, so grab them when you can and and stash this jam in your pantry.

2 pints (about 20) fresh figs, stemmed and chopped

2 Bosc pears, peeled, cored, and chopped

1/4 cup honey, preferably wildflower or lavender

1 tablespoon lemon juice, or more to taste

Pinch of kosher salt

1/2 teaspoon almond extract

2 tablespoons seedless blackberry jelly

Superfine sugar to taste

Pull out the largest shallow microwave-safe glass or ceramic dish you have so that the fruit can nestle in a single layer.

Combine the honey, lemon juice, salt, and almond extract and drizzle the mixture over the fruit. Dampen a length of paper towel and drape it over the dish. Cook the fruit on high for 10 minutes. At this point it should be quite soft. Remove the fruit from the dish with a slotted spoon, letting the juice drip back into the dish. Set it aside.

Stir the jelly into the juice and taste it to see how much sugar it needs. This is jam, don't forget, so it should be quite sweet. Return the liquid to the oven and reduce on high, checking every 3 minutes until you have a light syrupy glaze. If the reserved fruit has exuded juice while sitting aside, pour the juice into the syrup and reduce again. When the jam cools, it will congeal a bit more, so don't reduce the liquid to a sticky syrup.

Return the fruit to the syrup and give it a final taste. You can add more lemon juice or more sugar at this point to suit your palate.

When the mixture has cooled enough to put it in a food processor, pulse it on and off a few times to give it a good spreading consistency with pleasant texture.

Pack the jam in screw-top jars and refrigerate. It will keep for months.

VARIATION:

This same procedure also works well for blueberries, and at the height of the season they often sell baskets at two for the price of one. That's the time to make jam.

1½ pints blueberries, picked over and
   washed
1½ cups sugar

1 tablespoon cinnamon
1 teaspoon salt

 Place all the ingredients in a microwave-safe dish and cook on high for about 6 minutes or until the blueberries pop open. Remove them and proceed as per the previous recipe. Process half the mixture, leaving the other half whole for texture.

GINGER CARAMEL SAUCE

Makes 1 quart

With all of the glorious pastries and desserts available at my restaurant, the favorite was coffee ice cream with Ginger Caramel Sauce. You can find preserved ginger in some specialty food stores, or you can make your own (see Cook's Notes, page 159). Always heat the sauce in the microwave to pouring consistency before serving, as it will harden when it cools.

2½ cups brown sugar
1¼ cups corn syrup
2 tablespoons ginger syrup from jar
½ pound (2 sticks) butter

1 cup heavy cream
1 teaspoon pure vanilla extract
½ cup minced Preserved Ginger
   (page 159)

Cook the sugar, corn syrup, ginger syrup, and butter over low heat until the mixture reaches 240° on an instant-read or candy thermometer. Carefully stir in the remaining ingredients. Allow to cool enough to pour into screw-top jars for storage.

CHOCOLATE RUM SAUCE

Makes 2 cups

A good chocolate sauce speaks for itself, but I will add that the better the chocolate, the better the sauce.

8 ounces semisweet chocolate such as
    Lindt, Ghirardelli, or Valrhona
4 tablespoons (½ stick) butter

½ cup light cream or half and half,
    at room temperature
2 tablespoons dark rum

❧ Chop the chocolate into small pieces and combine all of the ingredients in a deep microwave-safe bowl or large glass measuring cup. Microwave on high for 5 minutes, checking after 3, and whisk the sauce to combine. Store in screw-top jars and refrigerate. Reheat briefly to serve. The sauce will keep for several weeks.

COOK'S NOTES: *You can use Kahlúa, framboise, brandy, or white crème de menthe in place of the rum. Remember, when melting chocolate in the microwave, it will still look solid when it's actually not. When you check it, push the chocolate with your spoon to see if it's soft enough to whisk. If you heat it too long it could seize, so be cautious.*

BLUEBERRY BRAN MUFFINS

Makes 12

Store-bought muffins are often too sweet, and the dough seems to dissolve into a gummy lump in your mouth. Add that to ersatz flavorings, canned fruit, and prices to knock your socks off, so it's silly not to make your own. Even devout nonbakers can make a good muffin. This one is moist and delicious and will keep at room temperature for 2 or 3 days if you heat them first in the toaster oven (never the microwave). Muffins freeze well in freezer bags for a week.

1 egg
1 cup plain yogurt (not nonfat)
1 teaspoon pure vanilla extract
6 tablespoons (³/₄ stick) butter, melted
³/₄ cup packed brown sugar
1 cup blueberries, picked over, washed, and dried

1 cup flour
1 cup unprocessed bran (*not bran flakes or cereal*)
1 teaspoon baking soda
1 teaspoon baking powder
1 teaspoon cinnamon

Preheat the oven to 375° and line a muffin tin with paper muffin cups.

Using a hand mixer or a whisk, combine the egg, yogurt, vanilla, butter, and sugar. Place the blueberries in a small bowl with a tablespoon of the flour and toss to lightly coat. In a separate bowl, whisk the flour, bran, baking soda, baking powder, and cinnamon.

Carefully combine the wet ingredients with the dry ingredients just until the flour disappears. Do not beat. Fold in the berries. Fill the muffin cups and bake for about 25 minutes or until a cake tester inserted in the top of a muffin comes out clean and dry.

TOASTED WALNUT SPICE MUFFINS

Makes 8

These muffins are truly worthy of a freshly brewed latte. Baked in paper muffin cups, they'll keep in a covered container for 2 to 3 days if reheated briefly in the toaster oven (never the microwave). They will also keep perfectly in a tightly sealed bag in the freezer for a week. The only problem is remembering to take some out the night before.

½ cup chopped walnuts or pecans
½ cup (1 stick) butter, at room
    temperature
1⅓ cups lightly packed brown sugar
2 eggs
¾ cup sour cream
1¼ cups flour

2 teaspoons baking powder
¼ teaspoon baking soda
2 teaspoons cinnamon
½ teaspoon ground ginger
½ teaspoon cloves
¼ teaspoon cardamom
¼ teaspoon salt

Preheat the oven to 375° and line a muffin tin with paper muffin cups. Toast the walnuts in a small skillet with a tablespoon of the butter. (They are done when you can smell their essence.)

In a standing mixer or food processor, cream the butter and sugar until there are no sugar lumps and the mixture is smooth. Add the eggs one at a time and blend well. The mixture should be fluffy.

Whisk the remaining ingredients in a medium mixing bowl to distribute the spices, and gently fold in the dry ingredients. Do not beat the mixture or your muffins will be tough. Fold in the toasted nuts.

Spoon the batter into the muffin cups and bake for about 25 minutes or until a cake tester pulls out of the center clean.

A COOKIE FOR ALL REASONS

Almond, Chocolate, Lemon, Ginger, Coconut, or Cinnamon | Makes 6 dozen

I can still see those plates of decorated Christmas tree–shaped spritz cookies my mom used to squeeze out and bake so effortlessly, which I loved with a glass of ice cold milk. A few years ago I bought a fancy imported press, and every Christmas since I've tried to use it. Darned if I can make that obstinate device work, but the recipe that I recall came in the cookie press box is a definite winner. It's crisp and buttery and takes to different flavors like a chameleon. This is the perfect dough to bag and store in the refrigerator or freezer for those days when the cookie monsters prowl.

3/4 pound (3 sticks) butter, at room temperature	1½ teaspoons pure vanilla extract
1 cup sugar	½ teaspoon almond extract
½ teaspoon kosher salt	2 egg yolks
	3¾ cups flour

❧ Preheat the oven to 350°. In a standing mixer or with a hand mixer, cream the butter and sugar until it's light and fluffy. Add the salt, extracts, and egg yolks and beat until smooth.

Incorporate the flour into the butter base until no floury patches remain.

Make a thumbprint cookie by lightly rolling a marble-size piece of dough between your palms and using your thumb to indent the center. Or, fill the cookie pan with the balls, about 1½ inches apart, and lay a sheet of plastic wrap on top. Press down lightly on each cookie with the bottom of a juice glass.

Bake 12 to 15 minutes until the edges of the cookies are golden. Cool on a rack.

COOK'S NOTES: *For a prettier cookie for guests, brush the tops with a wash of 1 egg white mixed with 2 teaspoons of water and sprinkle each with turbinado sugar.*

VARIATIONS:

Add 2 ounces melted and cooled chocolate to the butter/sugar base and omit the almond extract.

Add 1 tablespoon grated lemon zest. Use 1 teaspoon pure vanilla extract and ½ teaspoon each almond and lemon extracts. Add ⅓ cup finely chopped unsalted pistachios.

Add ⅓ cup finely minced crystallized ginger, ½ teaspoon ground ginger, and ½ teaspoon white pepper.

Use 1 teaspoon pure vanilla extract and 1 teaspoon natural coconut extract. Add ½ cup toasted coconut.

Use 2 teaspoons pure vanilla extract and substitute brown sugar for white Add 2 tablespoons cinnamon.

TOASTED NUTS AND COCONUT

How many times have you wished you had some toasted nuts when it's too late to turn the oven on and wait? Toast your favorite nuts and coconut on your weekend kitchen time and store them in screw-top jars in your refrigerator or freezer. They will also keep for at least a couple of weeks on the pantry shelf.

Bake the nuts in a 325° oven (the toaster oven works fine), shaking the pan several times until they release their distinct aroma and turn golden. (Don't stray from the kitchen, as nuts can burn during even the briefest phone call!) Coconut, however, is even worse. Watch it like a hawk, stirring in the browned edges often to get as even a toasting as you can.

Makes 12

*G*ood ideas will make the rounds, and this one started with Margaret Fox's Breakfast Cookies at Café Beaujolais in Mendocino, California. I've lost track of what was in the original recipe, but I remember being so charmed by the idea of having a big fat good-for-you cookie for breakfast that I headed straight for the kitchen to make my own. I keep changing the nut butter, cereal, and flavorings, depending on what's around, but this version is what's in my cookie jar as I write.

4 tablespoons (½ stick) butter, at room temperature
¼ cup safflower or canola oil
1 egg
⅓ cup almond butter
1 teaspoon almond extract
1 teaspoon pure vanilla extract
¾ cup lightly packed brown sugar

1 cup flour
½ teaspoon salt
¼ cup wheat germ
1 teaspoon baking powder
½ cup each Cheerios and Rice Krispies
½ cup chopped toasted almonds or ⅓ cup currants
12 whole unblanched almonds

Preheat the oven to 350° and line a cookie pan with parchment paper.

Place the butter, oil, egg, nut butter, extracts, and sugar in a food processor and puree until smooth. In a large bowl, whisk to combine the flour, salt, wheat germ, and baking powder. Add and mix in the wet ingredients and fold in the cereals and chopped nuts. (The dough will be stiff.)

Place golf-ball-size clumps of dough on the cookie pan, press a whole almond in the center of each cookie, and bake for 15 minutes or until the bottoms are light brown. Cool on a rack.

30-MINUTE LIME CHEESECAKE

Makes one 8-inch cake

Prep time isn't supposed to be an obstacle when you have a free day to cook, but when you want to add a treat, quick is a definite bonus. This is a very refreshing, light, untraditional cheesecake that pairs perfectly with a topping of mango slices or fresh pineapple soaked in rum. It's equally good totally unadorned.

½ cup finely crushed gingersnaps or
    graham crackers
1 cup large curd cottage cheese
1 cup sugar, preferably superfine
4 tablespoons (½ stick) butter, softened

3 eggs
Grated zest and juice of 1 lime
1 teaspoon pure vanilla extract
Several gratings of whole nutmeg

Preheat the oven to 400°. Lightly butter an 8-inch springform pan and coat lightly with the cookie crumbs all around.

Place the remaining ingredients in a food processor and combine until smooth. Pour the mixture into the prepared pan and bake for 30 minutes. Allow to cool and refrigerate the cake for 1 hour before removing from the pan.

APPLE and CURRANT SOUR CREAM PIE

Makes one 9-inch pie

This old-fashioned custardy apple pie with a streusel topping is a nice take on the purist's version of the apple pie we all love. If there's any left over, it keeps pretty well, on the counter for a couple days, or in the fridge a bit longer, if you must.

2 eggs
½ cup plus 1 tablespoon sugar
2 tablespoons flour
¼ teaspoon kosher salt
1 cup sour cream
1 teaspoon grated lemon zest
⅓ cup currants
2½ cups sliced peeled Golden Delicious apples

One 9-inch unbaked pie crust (recipe below)

The Topping:
½ cup flour
⅓ cup sugar
¼ teaspoon nutmeg
3 tablespoons butter

ᐷ Preheat the oven to 400°.

Beat the eggs until frothy and combine with the ½ cup sugar, flour, salt, sour cream, lemon zest, and currants. Toss the apples with the remaining 1 tablespoon sugar and a squeeze of lemon juice. Stir in the egg mixture. Fill the pie crust and bake for 10 minutes.

Meanwhile, combine the flour, sugar, and nutmeg for the topping and cut in the butter with two knives or your fingers. Sprinkle the streusel over the pie and bake for another 30 minutes at 375° until the topping is brown and the filling is set.

COOK'S NOTES: *You can also make this pie with blueberries. Omit the lemon zest and currants and combine ½ teaspoon cinnamon with the streusel sugar.*

PROCESSOR 2-CRUST PIE DOUGH

Makes two 9- or 10-inch pie crusts

3 cups all-purpose flour
½ cup (1 stick) very cold, or frozen, unsalted butter

½ cup very cold solid shortening (preferably Crisco)
½ teaspoon kosher salt
⅓ to ½ cup ice water

Place the flour, butter, shortening, and salt in a food processor and pulse on and off until the mixture is mealy with some visible pea-size lumps of shortening. Add ⅓ cup of ice water and pulse on and off again until you can see the dough is lightly moistened but has not started to form a cohesive ball. Pinch a little of the dough between your thumb and forefinger, and if it sticks together, the dough is ready; if it does not, add water 1 tablespoon at a time. Do not overmix.

Dump the dough out onto a lightly floured board and quickly press and pat it all together with your fingers into a smooth ball. Cut the dough into two equal pieces and flatten each one slightly. Wrap each piece in plastic wrap and freeze one for future use. Leave the other piece in the refrigerator for 30 minutes before attempting to roll it out.

After fitting the dough into a 9- or 10-inch pie pan, line it with a piece of foil weighted down with dried beans or pie weights and prebake in a preheated 400° oven for 10 minutes before adding the filling.

TRIPLE CHOCOLATE KEEPING CAKE

Makes 1 loaf

This is a recipe I pledged not to publish so I could mass-produce it and make my fortune. That was ten years ago, so I guess I'm not going into the cake-baking business any time soon. Drizzled with liqueur this cake will keep up to 2 weeks at room temperature, and it freezes well. It's a better gift alternative than Christmas cookies and a lot less work.

1¼ cups all-purpose flour

¾ cup granulated sugar

½ cup packed light brown sugar

6 tablespoons Dutch cocoa

2 teaspoons instant powdered espresso,
    preferably Medaglia D'Oro

1 teaspoon baking soda

¾ teaspoon kosher salt

1 cup mini–chocolate chips

1½ cups sour cream

1 egg

1½ teaspoons pure vanilla extract

4 tablespoons (½ stick) butter, melted
    and cooled

Kahlúa

 Preheat the oven to 350°. Butter a 9 x 5 x 3-inch loaf pan and dust it with flour, tapping out the excess. Line the bottom with parchment paper, press it down on the buttered pan, and flip it over so both sides are buttered.

Whisk to combine the flour, sugars, cocoa, coffee, baking soda, and salt. Stir in the chocolate chips. In a large bowl, whisk to combine the sour cream, egg, vanilla, and melted butter. Add the dry ingredients to the wet mixture with a rubber spatula, stirring until just blended and no flour appears. Spread evenly in the prepared pan. Bake 1 hour and 10 minutes, or until a cake tester pulls out clean. Cool the cake in the pan on a rack for 10 minutes. Turn it out of the pan and finish cooling on the rack. Wait several hours or overnight before drizzling the bottom of the cake with liqueur. Wrap in foil immediately.

THE CLASSY GRANITA

Makes 1 quart

My first experience with granita was not in its birthplace, Sicily, where it would have been impossible to divert me from ice cream. Rather, it was a few years ago at the late Jean-Louis Palladin's restaurant in Washington, D.C. It was one of those unforgettable culinary quick takes. Rising from the center of a frosted glass soup plate of satiny, coral-colored cream of carrot soup was an iceberg of crimson red tomato granita. Brilliant.

Granita has since become the restaurant chef's favorite both as an intermezzo and as dessert, and no wonder: It's a snap to make, and inventive flavor combinations are endless. Try some of these any time of year and you'll be hooked.

LEMON COCONUT
1½ cups each sugar and water, plus 1 additional cup water
2 cups fresh lemon juice
1 tablespoon grated lemon zest
¼ cup coconut rum or light rum, and
    ½ teaspoon coconut extract (optional)
½ teaspoon pure vanilla extract

Boil the sugar and 1½ cups water for 1 minute to dissolve the sugar; let cool. Combine all of the ingredients, plus 1 additional cup of water, and pour into a 9-inch square metal cake pan. Freeze for 2 hours; the mixture will have formed ice crystals around the edges. Scrape the sides and bottom of the pan toward the center and return to the freezer. Check every hour or so and scrape the frozen sections with a fork to fluff them up. Repeat until the granita is transformed into a pile of icy shards. Pile the granita into lidded containers and store in the freezer.

ESPRESSO KAHLÚA
3 cups water
½ cup sugar
1½ cups espresso, cooled
¼ teaspoon cinnamon
¼ cup Kahlúa

🎔 Proceed to prepare and freeze as instructed on page 173. Serve topped with whipped cream and shaved chocolate.

CRANBERRY-ORANGE BRANDY

3½ cups cranberry juice
¼ cup frozen orange juice concentrate
3 tablespoons brandy (optional)
¼ cup corn syrup, or to taste

🎔 Combine all the ingredients and proceed to freeze, scraping and fluffing, as previously instructed. Garnish each serving with Candied Orange Peel (page 159).

PINK GRAPEFRUIT

⅓ cup sugar
⅔ cup water
2 cups ruby grapefruit juice with some of the pulp
1 tablespoon grated grapefruit zest
Mint sprigs for garnish

🎔 Combine the sugar and water and simmer over low heat until the sugar dissolves and the syrup is clear. Add the juice and zest, taste to adjust the sweetness level, and simmer for 5 minutes. Do not boil or reduce. Allow to cool and freeze according to previous instructions. Garnish with mint sprigs.

CHÈVRE CHEESECAKE with HERBS

Serves 8

Here's a canapé that can be made 2 or 3 days ahead and served with crackers, although the cake is firm enough to be cut in small wedges and served without them. You could also cut it into fingers and place one to the side of a mesclun salad for an inviting first course.

½ pound plain or peppered chèvre
⅓ cup small-curd cottage cheese
2 tablespoons soft butter
2 eggs
Pinch of kosher salt
Pinch of cayenne pepper

2 teaspoons pureed Roasted Garlic
  (page 155)
¾ cup minced mixed herbs, such as
  parsley, chives, thyme, savory,
  and basil
½ cup fine dry bread or cracker crumbs

∾ Preheat the oven to 375°. Butter an 8-inch springform pan and coat it with the crumbs.

Combine all the remaining ingredients in a food processor until smooth. Pour the mixture into the prepared pan and bake for 30 minutes until the cake is firm.

OLIVE CHEESE BITES

Makes 25

There are a few oldies that are such goodies they deserve to survive. My mother made these often for cocktail parties, and I used to snitch them from the tray before they made it to the living room. I was a strange child who loved olives—even those awful canned ripe ones Mom was forced to use. I still have her handwritten recipe card that says it takes an hour to make 50 cheese bites.

The exact number you will get depends on the size of the olive. If you buy the colossal stuffed green olives, your guests will need a knife and fork, so select your olives carefully. If you can find pitted Kalamatas, you can tuck a sliver of scallion inside or a sliver of poached garlic, anchovy, or toasted almond. You can also stuff pitted green olives with a little pickled jalapeño, or use the small pimiento-stuffed ones. The finished bites will keep in the refrigerator for a day or two before baking, or you could freeze them on a tray and store in plastic bags. They needn't be thawed before baking; just increase the baking time to about 25 minutes.

25 pitted and stuffed olives
   (see suggestions above)
1/2 cup sifted flour
1/8 teaspoon dry mustard
1/8 teaspoon salt
1/8 teaspoon cayenne pepper

1/8 teaspoon black pepper, freshly
   ground
1 cup grated sharp Cheddar
3 tablespoons melted butter
1 teaspoon milk

ɔ Preheat the oven to 400°.

Whisk or sift together the dry ingredients until thoroughly combined. Stir in the cheese, butter, and milk. Mold a rounded teaspoon of the mixture around each olive with your fingers, covering the olive completely. Bake 12 to 14 minutes. Serve warm.

SOUR CREAM TURNOVER PASTRY

This is the sensational dough for *Lihamurekepiiras* (page 68) that I'm including here because it has multiple uses for savory canapé turnovers. It's a handy, user-friendly dough to keep in the freezer or to make ahead and store in the refrigerator.

You can stuff bite-size or larger turnovers with Caramelized Onions (page 126); Garlic Mushrooms with Frizzled Prosciutto (page 128); Holiday Cranberry Chutney (page 137); Bolognese Meat Sauce (page 150); Eggplant Ragout (page 103); West Indian Red Beans (page 113) or one of the ground meat or stuffing mixtures in chapter 3.

2¼ cups flour, sifted

¾ teaspoon salt

12 tablespoons (1½ sticks) butter,
   cut into small cubes

1 egg

½ cup sour cream

꙼ Place the flour, salt, and butter in a food processor and pulse on and off until the mixture resembles a coarse meal with some pea-size pieces of butter remaining.

Whisk the egg and sour cream together in a large bowl and stir into it the flour/butter mixture. Work quickly with your fingers to bring the dough together into a soft, pliable ball. Refrigerate for 1 hour before rolling.

SPICY MAPLE WALNUTS

Serves 12

These nuts are truly addictive, so if you're making them for company or as gifts, I suggest you double the recipe so you'll have some for family treats.

1 pound walnuts, 4 cups

4 tablespoons (½ stick) unsalted butter

¼ cup pure maple syrup

6 quarter-size slices of fresh gingerroot, slivered

1 teaspoon ground ginger

1 tablespoon water

1 teaspoon salt

¼ teaspoon Tabasco, or to taste

Preheat the oven to 300°. Line a jelly roll pan with foil.

Place the nuts in a large bowl. Combine the remaining ingredients in a saucepan and simmer over low heat for 2 to 3 minutes. Pour the glaze over the nuts and toss to coat. Spread the nuts in a single layer in the prepared pan and bake for 15 minutes.

Toss the nuts with a large metal spoon, thoroughly recoating them with the glaze. Bake in two more 10-minute increments, scooping up the glaze each time to cover the nuts. (By now the glaze will be quite sticky and easier to scrape up onto the nuts.) Watch them closely for another 10 minutes, at which point the nuts will feel light and almost dry.

The nuts will continue to toast from the intense heat of the sugar glaze, so be careful not to overbake and don't touch them with your fingers. Slide the foil out onto a cooling rack and allow the nuts to cool completely before prying them off the foil and storing in screw-top jars or in an airtight tin. Leave the ginger strips in for a spicy surprise, but if you store the nuts too long the ginger can become hard to chew.

MALABAR PECANS

Serves 12

These nuts are everyone's favorite, so don't expect to have leftovers. If you have any home-made Curry Powder (page 123), by all means use it in place of the store-bought Madras curry called for here. You can delete the garam masala in that case.

4 tablespoons (½ stick) unsalted butter

2 tablespoons safflower or canola oil

1 tablespoon Madras curry powder
   (see headnote above)

2 teaspoons garam masala
   (see headnote above)

½ teaspoon ground cumin

2 teaspoons cinnamon

1 tablespoon salt

¼ teaspoon cayenne pepper

1 pound pecan halves, 4 cups

 Preheat the oven to 300°. Line a jelly roll pan with foil.

Heat all of the ingredients except the nuts in a small skillet over medium heat. Place the nuts in a large bowl and pour the seasoning over them, tossing to coat. Spread the nuts out in a single layer in the pan and bake for 30 minutes, stirring at ten-minute intervals. When the nuts are very aromatic and deeply brown, remove them from the oven and slide the foil out onto a cooling rack.

When the nuts are cool enough to taste, you can adjust the seasoning by dusting the nuts with additional curry, cayenne, and salt.

FRESH CHOCOLATE TRUFFLES

Makes 3 dozen

Making your own truffles can unveil some of their mystery and lead you to believe there's nothing to it. It's true that even with little experience working with chocolate you can achieve a decent facsimile of a great chocolatier's creations, but a sublime fresh truffle is another matter. Success is in the subtleties.

That said, this recipe is quite simple. All you need is quality chocolate, which doesn't mean the most expensive; Ghirardelli and Lindt Excellence brands will work well. For a longer life, ultrapasteurized cream is best.

By all means, separate the batch into two or three parts so you can flavor and coat each one differently. And don't forget to present the truffles to your guests decorated with an assortment of Candied Citrus Peel (page 159).

3/4 cup heavy cream (see headnote above)

12 ounces bittersweet or semisweet chocolate, finely chopped

4 tablespoons (1/2 stick) unsalted butter

Pinch of kosher salt

3 tablespoons of liqueur (see Flavoring Suggestions below)

Confectioners' sugar (see Coating Suggestions, page 181)

In a saucepan, bring the cream just to the point of boiling and remove from the heat. Add the chocolate and stir until the mixture is completely melted and smooth. Allow the mixture to cool slightly before stirring in the butter 1 tablespoon at a time. Add a pinch of salt and stir again.

Either add 3 tablespoons of one liqueur or divide the chocolate into three bowls and add 1 tablespoon of three different liqueurs. Cover the mixtures and chill until very firm, about 2 to 3 hours.

Prepare the truffle coatings on separate plates. Dust your hands with confectioners' sugar, scoop the chocolate up with a melon baller or a teaspoon, and form irregular balls with your fingers. Drop them on the plate of coating and when you finish all the balls, roll them around on the plate with a fork to coat thoroughly.

Pack the truffles between sheets of wax paper in an airtight container. Refrigerate for 2 weeks or freeze for a month.

FLAVORING SUGGESTIONS:

Brandy, rum, Grand Marnier, Chambord, Kahlúa, Peppermint Schnapps, Irish Mist

COATING SUGGESTIONS:

Toasted coconut, Dutch cocoa mixed with confectioners' sugar, chocolate jimmies, finely chopped toasted nuts, crushed chocolate-covered espresso beans, five cookie crumbs

ALTERNATIVE CHOCOLATE COATING:

You don't need to use tempered chocolate to cover the truffles, but if you don't, they won't have that professional sheen or snap to the bite, and you risk smeary fingers if they get too warm. A good compromise to tempering is to add a couple of teaspoons of shortening to the warm dipping chocolate and use a wooden skewer to hold the truffle for dipping. Chill the truffles to set the coating.

A TRUFFLE TREAT FOR THE KIDS:

Combine 1 cup semisweet chocolate chips, ¼ cup heavy cream, 1 teaspoon pure vanilla extract, 3 tablespoons chunky peanut butter, and 1 tablespoon butter in a small saucepan and stir over moderate heat until smooth. Chill until firm and roll the truffles in finely chopped salted peanuts.

Index

Metric Equivalencies

Liquid and Dry Measure Equivalencies

CUSTOMARY	METRIC
¼ teaspoon	1.25 milliliters
½ teaspoon	2.5 milliliters
1 teaspoon	5 milliliters
1 tablespoon	15 milliliters
1 fluid ounce	30 milliliters
¼ cup	60 milliliters
⅓ cup	80 milliliters
½ cup	120 milliliters
1 cup	240 milliliters
1 pint *(2 cups)*	480 milliliters
1 quart *(4 cups, 32 ounces)*	960 milliliters *(.96 liter)*
1 gallon *(4 quarts)*	3.84 liters
1 ounce *(by weight)*	28 grams
¼ pound *(4 ounces)*	114 grams
1 pound *(16 ounces)*	454 grams
2.2 pounds	1 kilogram *(1,000 grams)*

Oven-Temperature Equivalencies

DESCRIPTION	°FAHRENHEIT	°CELSIUS
Cool	200	90
Very slow	250	120
Slow	300–325	150–160
Moderately slow	325–350	160–180
Moderate	350–375	180–190
Moderately hot	375–400	190–200
Hot	400–450	200–230
Very hot	450–500	230–260